CASE STUDIES IN
CULTURAL ANTHROPOLOGY

GENERAL EDITORS
George and Louise Spindler
STANFORD UNIVERSITY

THE ESKIMO OF NORTH ALASKA

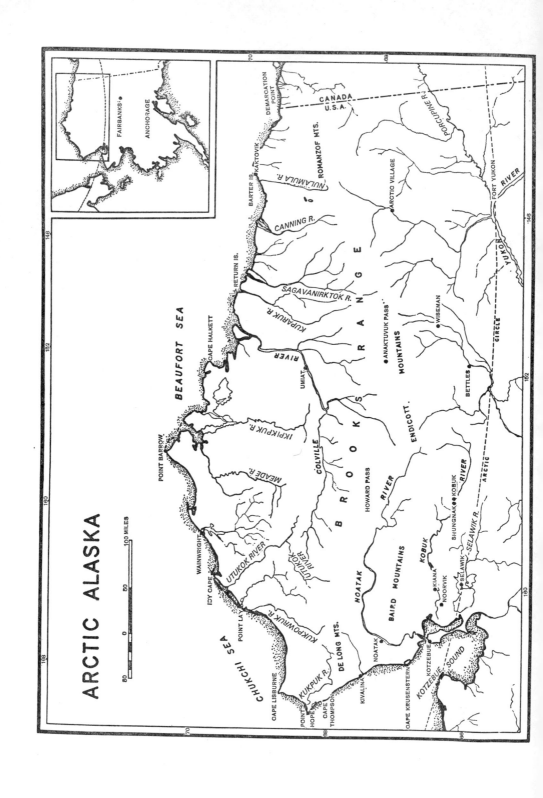

THE ESKIMO
OF NORTH ALASKA

By

NORMAN A. CHANCE
McGill University

HOLT, RINEHART AND WINSTON
NEW YORK   CHICAGO   SAN FRANCISCO   TORONTO   LONDON

To Nancy

Foreword

About the Series

These case studies in cultural anthropology are designed to bring to students in the social sciences insights into the richness and complexity of human life as it is lived in different ways and in different places. They are written by men and women who have lived in the societies they write about, and who are professionally trained as observers and interpreters of human behavior. The authors are also teachers, and in writing their books they have kept the students who will read them foremost in their minds. It is our belief that when an understanding of ways of life very different from one's own is gained, abstractions and generalizations about social structure, cultural values, subsistence techniques, and other universal categories of human social behavior become meaningful.

About the Author

Norman A. Chance is Associate Professor of Anthropology and Director of the Program in the Anthropology of Development at McGill University, Montreal, Canada. He was born in Lynn, Massachusetts, and studied anthropology at the University of Pennsylvania before receiving his Ph.D. degree from Cornell University in 1957. He taught previously at the University of Oklahoma, held postdoctoral research fellowships from the Russell Sage Foundation, Harvard University, and the Arctic Institute of North America, and conducted field research in the southwest United States, Alaska, Mexico, and Puerto Rico. He is a fellow of the American Anthropological Association, the Society for Applied Anthropology, and the American Association for the Advancement of Science. He is a coeditor of *Transcultural Psychiatric Research* and the author of numerous articles dealing with problems of culture change and applied anthropology.

About the Book

This is a case study of the modern Eskimo. The Eskimo of the outboard motor, electric lights, fuel-oil heat, canned goods, clinic and hospital care, Levis and jackets, and the twist. But it is also a study of a people who still hunt walrus, seal, and whales, who wear caribou parkas, and who observe the *nalukatak* (spring whale festival) each year. The old Eskimo way is in some areas of life intertwined with the new ways borrowed from the *tannik* (white man) and in other areas it lies just beneath the surface. The people are both modern and traditional in their behavior, attitudes, and thinking. They are pragmatists who use what is available to them. They adapt to the white man, and the goods and services his way of life provides, as they have adapted to their own natural environment and its resources. They are a people whose technology has changed and is changing, and whose social forms and belief systems are reforming along new lines. They are also a people whose self-image is shifting toward more full participation in the stream of Western culture and world affairs.

Norman Chance has handled a difficult task well. He has given us both an understanding of the change and flux of modern Alaskan Eskimo life and an insight into the character of traditional life.

GEORGE AND LOUISE SPINDLER
General Editors

Stanford, California
April 1966

Preface

The field work on which this monograph is based was conducted between the years 1958 and 1962 in Barrow, Kaktovik, and Wainwright, Alaska, during the summers of 1958, 1961, 1962, and part of the winter of 1960. The author spent the summer of 1958, part of the months of March and April 1960, and most of August 1962 in Kaktovik. Miss Jean Briggs, research assistant on the project, spent the summer of 1961 at Kaktovik and the following summer at Wainwright with a two week visit to Kaktovik. Supplementary field work at Barrow was done by both anthropologists during short periods en route to and from the other two villages.

I am very grateful to the Arctic Institute of North America, the United States Office of Naval Research, and the National Institute of Mental Health for the financial support which made the field study and preparation of this monograph possible. Invaluable aid has also been given by the director, Dr. Max Brewer, and staff of the Arctic Research Laboratory, Barrow, Alaska; the Arctic Health Research Center of the United States Public Health Service; and the Russell Sage Foundation.

A special debt of gratitude must go to Jean Briggs, without whose assistance this monograph would not have been undertaken. Much of the written material concerning child-rearing practices and the changing role of women was largely drawn from her insightful reporting and analysis, and the results of her stimulating and creative efforts appear in many other sections as well.

To Dr. Margaret Lantis, whose help and advice has been sought many times throughout the course of the study, I offer my appreciation.

Helpful comments on various sections of the monograph also have been received from Donald Foote, John Honigmann, James VanStone, and William N. Irving.

Editorial and typing assistance were ably given by Page Porter and Alice Gutkind.

Finally, I wish to thank Mrs. Berit Armstad Foote, who contributed the fine drawings of village scenes based on her years of residence at Point Hope, Alaska.

The current trend in anthropology and social science in general is to study the regularities in human behavior and the social patterns which are abstracted from this behavior. Although this approach is an acceptable one, it must be borne in mind that the source of all theories and abstractions in these disciplines is human beings, who have their individual emotions, subjective attitudes, reactions, and motivations.

Since the anthropologist is a human being studying other human beings, he must be particularly careful to undertake his research with as much objectivity as possible, interview a significant cross section of the population, and keep his subjective thoughts and comments to himself. In spite of this care, so-called cultural bias is seldom, if ever, completely absent from the investigator's report. Field work among any group of people is always a very personal experience. Among the Eskimo it was also a richly rewarding one. It is only fair, therefore, that I preface this book by stating that the qualities of warmth, good humor, friendliness, and generosity shown by the north Alaskan Eskimo have thoroughly tested this anthropologist's ability to be objective.

N. A. C.

Montréal, Canada
April 1966

Contents

The Eskimo of North Alaska

Introduction

O NE OF MAN'S most significant attributes is his ability to comprehend his own past. By learning facts about our origins and understanding the variety of ways in which we have developed, students of human history have slowly accumulated a vast knowledge of our physical and cultural heritage. Anthropology, as the comparative study of man, has set as one of its major goals the discovery of similarities and differences in human behavior among the societies of the world.

Involved in the rapid technological and social revolutions that have swept around the globe in the past few decades, Western man hardly need be reminded of the differences that obtain in racial type, social behavior, and cultural beliefs and values; they are all about him. He does sometimes forget the equally important physical and cultural similarities that mankind shares. Not only do we belong to the same species—a fairly recent phenomenon in the history of human evolution, but we also share with men everywhere a common core of basic problems.

All peoples of the world must deal with their physical environment in such a manner that they can obtain sufficient food, clothing, and the other essentials of life; learn to control their relations with others in an orderly fashion; develop a set of values and beliefs that give coherence to their actions; and provide for the care and training of their children. It is because these and other problems are essentially the same the world over that we can speak meaningfully about the economic, political, religious, educational, and other universal human institutions. Still, the many problems posed by man's basic biopsychological make-up seldom exact similar answers, and the great variety of cultural solutions to universal problems has interested the anthropologist since the founding of the discipline.

This ethnographic study of the north Alaskan Eskimo will demonstrate how one group of people has solved the problem of survival—the most basic of all universal problems—in one of the harshest environments known to man. Sustaining human life in the low-temperature regions of the far north raises problems of a kind found nowhere else in the world; yet, as any Western school-age child knows, the Eskimo have not only adapted to this environment by means of the igloo, fur clothing, kayak, dog sled, harpoon, and other ingenious items of technology, but they usually prefer it to any other. What is perhaps less well known is how the nonmaterial elements of Eskimo culture, particularly their social structure and belief system, have been equally well adapted to traditional problems of life in the arctic.

For many years the Eskimo lived in a world of relative stability where, given the techniques they had developed, they could adjust to their northern environment indefinitely. The changes that did occur in their technology and social life did little to disrupt this stability, and each new generation could predict with a fair degree of accuracy the course its future would follow. Furthermore, when these predictions were not realized, the culture provided other mechanisms to deal with this failure.

To take one example: throughout much of their history the Eskimo have faced continually the problem of an unstable food supply. With their level of technology and in the environment in which they lived, it was impossible to ensure a sufficient surplus of food to last each family throughout every winter. The Eskimo partially solved this problem by requiring that much of the food be shared, particularly among extended kin. Fatalism, a traditional Eskimo value, played a part in the adjustment process in that it relieved some of the pressure on the unsuccessful hunter and his family. While the physiological feeling of hunger was not lessened, it was at least tempered by a reduction in feelings of frustration. Traditional Eskimo religious beliefs could also be called upon to "explain" a temporary loss of food supply: a kin member had broken an important taboo or an evil spirit had driven away the game.

Further examples of the interrelatedness of technology, social life, and cultural life are discussed below, demonstrating that among the aboriginal Eskimo the social structure and belief system in combination provided a generally effective, albeit imperfect, solution to many of the basic problems brought on by life in an arctic environment with a limited technology.

As explorers, whalers, and other whites moved north, the Eskimo world changed dramatically. The introduction of the rifle, iron and steel implements, drugs and medicines, and other items of Western manufacture resolved many of the earlier technological problems of the Eskimo; this in turn, stimulated changes in other spheres of their life. Although the use of the rifle made hunting easier, it reduced the need for sharing and cooperation among kin groups, lessened the prestige of the hunter, and brought into question the validity of the traditional religion by raising doubts about the importance of certain rituals and taboos connected with hunting. This questioning of religion affected the traditional means of social control in that the threat of supernatural punishment for deviation from approved Eskimo practices lost much of its force. As we trace the history of the north Alaskan Eskimo, we will learn how these people have attempted to deal with these and similar problems. Some solutions are uniquely Eskimo; others bear a strong resemblance to those arrived at by all peoples undergoing modernization; and still others are only temporary.

It is also important to consider the extent to which the external trappings of Western society—the purchase of Western goods and services, the building of Western-style houses, the participation in Western games and other activities—have significantly modified the Eskimo's self-image. Are those Eskimo who adopt Western forms of behavior complying with the wishes of an outside group in order to achieve a favorable response useful in the attainment of their traditional goals? Many Eskimo imitate Western models of behavior and use its material goods because these items provide a refreshing change in the day-to-day life of the village, or simply because they make life easier. To what extent, if at all, do these innovations affect their self-image? Do these actions reflect a new self-identification in which the Eskimo see themselves as becoming a part of the Western world? The answers to these questions are complex and they vary among individuals in different circumstances. But the subject of identity should be considered in any account of the Eskimo, for as he gains more technical control over his physical environment he gains greater freedom of choice in his actions; and the choices he makes depend in part on how he sees himself in relation to others.

In the chapters that follow we begin by examining how the Eskimo lived prior to extensive Western contact, and how this contact has modified their way of life. We then trace the Eskimo child from birth through infancy, childhood, and adolescence, when he begins to assume the roles and responsibilities of an adult. We learn how the Eskimo obtain their living, how they handle social relationships with others in the community, and how their cultural beliefs and values give coherence to their actions.

Equipped with this knowledge, the reader should then be prepared to undertake an analysis of the changing world of the north Alaskan Eskimo. Also discussed are important social, cultural, and psychological barriers and stimulants to change, focusing on problems of village integration, conflicting values, changing aspirations, self-identity, and government-Eskimo relations.

1

Innupiat: The Genuine People

FROM THE WINDOW of the small plane I looked down on the flat expanse of tundra 1000 feet below. Small streams and ice-filled lakes added brilliant contrast to the treeless landscape. The surrounding ground was covered with varieties of lichens, sedges, and mosses, giving the whole region a meadowlike appearance. Through the other window my eye followed the curving shore line of the north Alaskan coast over a stretch of open water to the white outline of the pack ice beyond. Beside me, the grey-haired man with bronzed Mongoloid features raised his hand and pointed toward a spit of land jutting out into the sea.

"Brownlow Point. Nobody lives there now."

Brownlow Point. The abandoned coastal settlement was clearly visible from the air. Several old houses were clustered a few yards back from the beach. Weathered walls still supported the occasional door and window frames, although the sod roofs had long since disappeared. Near one of the houses the huge sun-bleached skull of a whale lay half covered in the sand, and behind that rose a mound of stone topped by a wooden cross.

"Did any Kaktovik people ever live here?" I asked the old Eskimo sitting beside me. Ataatarurug once had spent many years in this part of north Alaska before returning to Barrow village, his original home. We both were now heading for the coastal village of Kaktovik, located on Barter Island, 300 miles east of Point Barrow, where he wanted to visit his daughter and other relatives, and I was to undertake a study of the community.

"Some Kaktovik people lived here once, but they moved away maybe forty or thirty years ago. Now only one Eskimo family lives between Barrow and Barter Island. Not very crowded, is it?" He looked at me, with a smile on his face.

"Not any more." Lapsing into silence I thought about the 1880s when over 500 Eskimo used to meet for trading at the mouth of the Colville River, west of Brownlow Point. Other abandoned camps and villages were scattered along this part of the coast, some dating back several hundred years.

Ten minutes later the pilot of the plane turned his radio compass to a new frequency and made a position report.

"Cessna 391 over Arey Island. Request permission to land at Barter Island. Have two passengers for the village."

Receiving approval, the man at the controls reduced the plane's throttle and began the long glide toward a gravel sand spit that reached out for several miles along the coast. At the near end of the spit on a high bluff were thirty or more houses of conglomerate shapes and sizes. Some were rough one-room board dwellings with a single small window to let in the light. Others formed long narrow lines. A few had been painted recently, but most were a dull shade of weathered grey. A parka-clad woman was hanging long thin strips of meat from drying racks constructed of driftwood and rope. Near here several children had just finished raising a small white canvas tent to sleep in during the coming summer. I recognized, about 100 yards beyond the village on a high knoll, the H-shaped building and large plastic dome of a new radar installation.

Banking sharply, the plane turned into the wind and began its final approach. As the wheels touched down on the gravel, small rocks slapped against the underside of the plane. Recognizing our startled looks, the pilot gave Ataatarurug and me a reassuring word.

"Here we are. I'll give you a hand with your gear. Then I've got to go up to the radar site for a bite and some gas before I head back. The radio operator says somebody from the village needs a ride to the Barrow hospital."

The Modern Eskimo

Today most north Alaskan Eskimo live in fairly large year-round coastal villages. From east to west, these communities are Kaktovik, located in the northeast corner of Alaska near the Canadian border; Barrow, a large village of more than 1200 people, situated at the northern tip of the state; Wainwright, 100 miles southwest of Barrow; and Point Hope, another 100 miles down the coast. With the exception of Barrow, these villages range in size from 100 to approximately 300 residents. A few other Eskimo live in smaller settlements, such as Point Lay and Kivalina, along the coast. The only truly inland north Alaskan Eskimo are the Nunamiut (People of the Land), a small group of related families who live in the Anaktuvuk Pass region of the Brooks Range and along the Kobuk and Noatak rivers. They are the last remnants of more than 3000 Nunamiut who once lived in the mountains and along the inland river system of northern Alaska.

The approximately 2500 north Alaskan Eskimo comprise only a small portion of Alaska's total Eskimo population of 28,600 (Bureau of Indian Affairs estimate). Most are found in the western half of the state. The largest population cluster is located in the area between Bristol Bay and Norton Sound, with the Seward Peninsula constituting the second major center. Although the latest census figure gives Barrow village a total population of 1215, fewer Eskimo live there than in the mixed Eskimo and white community of Nome. The linguistically related Aleut, with a population of 5700 live on the Alaska Peninsula and the Aleutian Islands.

These Alaskan Eskimo represent somewhat less than half of the more than 73,000 Eskimo presently distributed in extreme northeastern Siberia, and across Alaska and Canada to Greenland. Physical characteristics vary among the groups, but there are enough similarities in such discrete morphological traits as the mandibular torus, keel-shaped vault, and the inverted gonial angles to justify their being classified as a subgroup of the major Mongoloid racial stock.

The Eskimo linguistic stock is divided into two major branches, Eskimo proper and Aleut. Aleut belongs to the Eskimo, but it is a distinct language, and there are several other distinct dialects spoken as well. The linguist Morris Swadesh has divided the Eskimo language into two major divisions: Yupik, which includes the Siberian and southwest Alaskan dialects, and Inyupik, which includes the more northern dialects as found at Cape Prince of Wales, Point Barrow, Mackenzie, Coronation Gulf, and east to Greenland.

Eskimo settlement patterns vary according to region. Most of the Alaskan and Greenland Eskimo live in fairly permanent villages or settlements in winter and occasionally move to temporary hunting and fishing camps during the summer. On the other hand, many Eskimo of the Canadian arctic have until recently been much more nomadic, living in winter in temporary snowhouses built on sea ice, at fish camps in the summer, and roaming the interior to hunt caribou in the fall and spring.

Of these three major Eskimo groups, the central Canadian often is described as the most "typical." In terms of ceremonialism, art, and the variety and technical skill of their handicrafts, their culture is considered by many to be less complex than that of either the Alaskan or Greenland Eskimo. This simplicity is due largely to the severity of their high arctic environment where food, driftwood, and other natural resources are so limited that the people have had less opportunity to develop culturally. In this geographic area, life at a modest level has always required maximum effort.

The Alaskan Eskimo, in contrast, have had much more favorable environmental conditions at their disposal. The abundance of sea mammals and other marine life, in combination with large numbers of caribou and birds, has made Alaska one of the richer hunting regions of the world. Thus it is not surprising that the Alaskan Eskimo area has been more densely populated than any other, and its culture more elaborate than that of most other Eskimo groups. The Eskimo have used the ecology of north Alaska to their maximum advantage.

The Ecological Setting

A striking geographic feature of northern Alaska is the mountain chain that runs east and west from The Alaskan-Canadian boundary to the Chukchi Sea. Called the Brooks Range, these mountains form a continental divide, one set of streams flowing north to the sea and the rest flowing south and west to join the great river systems of central Alaska. The Brooks Range also separates the flat treeless tundra of the far north from the forested lands of the central Alaskan plateau. These mountains have an average height of 3000 feet in the west and reach more than 9000 feet near the Canadian boundary. Though rugged, craggy, and still marked by small glaciers, the range does have several well-defined passes through which caribou make their annual migrations. Man, too, has long inhabited these migration routes although only recently have archeologists gained any appreciable understanding of his early patterns of life.

The geographic area which is our primary concern extends from the Brooks Range north to the Arctic Ocean, west to Point Hope, and east to Demarcation Point. Called the arctic slope of Alaska, it includes the northern foothills of the Brooks Range and a low coastal plain. The coastal plain, varying in width from a few miles in the east to more than seventy miles in the west, is typical arctic tundra. In summer broad streams and rivers meander aimlessly through it before emptying into the sea. Shallow lakes and marshes cover much of the landscape. Except for numerous hummocks and knolls, the entire area is uniformly flat. An early explorer and geologist, Ernest Leffingwell, described it as being so featureless "that there are many places in which one would become lost without a compass." The slope of the land is so gradual that from a boat several miles out to sea, the coast line is hardly visible. Even the Eskimo, who know the coast thoroughly, will on occasion confuse one stream or point of land with another.

The north Alaskan tundra frequently has been referred to as a desert, and with good reason. The rain and snowfall in the region averages less than ten inches per year. Were it not for the perennially frozen topsoil and the permanently frozen subsoil (permafrost) preventing most underground drainage, a real desert would soon form. In addition to the permafrost and the horizontal plane of the land, another factor responsible for the accumulation of melted snow and rain is the relatively small amount of evaporation which results from the low angle of the sun.

The principal factors that distinguish the seasons are the length of daylight and the degree of temperature. At Point Barrow, for example, the average winter temperature ranges from −20° to −30°F, which, were it not for the severe wind, would compare favorably with the colder temperatures of −50° to −60° in interior Alaska. In summer, the temperature seldom drops below freezing and occasionally reaches as high as 60° to 70°F. An average of 40° to 45° is common in July.

Of equal importance is the dramatic change in hours of sunlight. During the brief arctic summer the sun shines almost continually for two months. In the fall there is a maximum of twelve hours of sunshine per day, followed by the complete absence of sun in mid-winter. Beginning around November 15, Point Barrow has seventy-two days without sun. There is sufficient refraction, however, during many of these days to provide a short period of daylight. With the coming of spring the sun again rises for increasing periods each day until the annual cycle is completed.

Along the north Alaskan coast, the prevailing wind is easterly, except for the winter months, when it blows from a northeasterly direction. This wind is one of the determinants of ice movement and all coastal navigation depends on its vagaries. The polar ice pack usually recedes from the region of Point Barrow by the first of August, and somewhat earlier to the east and west. Small boats can navigate in the leads formed between the shore and the pack ice by late spring and early summer. However, the movement of the ice is always a hazard and many boats, large and small, have been lost as the result of miscalculations.

By the middle of September, the pack ice moves closer to the coast and all navigation halts. New ice forming at this time prevents even small boats like the Eskimo umiak from putting out to sea, for the slush ice quickly blocks the passages. It is not until the middle of November that the new ice is of sufficient strength to support a sled and dog team, the traditional form of winter transportation. River ice usually breaks up in May or June, followed by the coastal ice in June or July.

Except for a few stunted willows growing in the river valleys and plateau region, there are no trees north of the Brooks Range. In the interior foothills, the willows may reach ten or fifteen feet in height, but near the coast they are rare and seldom stand higher than twelve inches. Throughout the summer a profusion of flowers of the rose, anemone, mustard, saxifrage, and aster families carpet much of the tundra. Grasses, mosses, sedges, and lichens add green and grey hues to this richly colored pattern.

Plant life available for human consumption has always been severely limited in north Alaska. In the foothills and along the slopes of the Brooks Range the many species and varieties of berries that flourish occasionally were picked and eaten. Mixed with caribou fat or seal oil, or pounded into pemmican, these berries were at one time an important trade item between the inland and coastal Eskimo. With the loss of the inland population, this trading pattern disappeared, and only rarely will a coastal Eskimo bring back cloudberries or other plant food from an inland hunting trip.

Wild animal life, in contrast, usually has been abundant. The caribou, traveling in herds through the passes of the Brooks Range to the coastal plain, were essential to the continued existence of the inland Eskimo, and still are a vital source of food for the maritime population. The Dall or mountain sheep, polar bear, and occasional arctic grizzly and moose provide a secondary source of meat. Several hundred years ago a few musk ox grazed in Alaska, but due to their peculiar defensive habits (when attacked they gather in a circle and stand immobile) they may have been killed off easily by man. The last musk ox in Alaska appears to have disappeared about 1860. Other land mammals are the fox, wolf, wolverine, arctic hare, squirrel, lynx, the smaller marmot, vole, and lemming. During the spring, summer, and fall, large flocks of birds such as the ptarmigan, duck, and goose inhabit the coastal region and offer the Eskimo another important food supplement.

Of greatest significance to the life of the coastal Eskimo is the availability of sea mammals. The most impressive in size are the immense bowhead whale, measuring from forty-five to sixty feet in length. These animals make annual migrations along the western coast of north Alaska from Point Hope to Point Barrow and eastward into the Beaufort Sea. The smaller beluga or "white whale" follow much the same summer route as the bowhead. Walrus and *ugrook* (large bearded seal) are common to the northwest coast, and less so east of Point Barrow. The most numerous and widespread sea mammals are the ringed, bearded, and harbor seal. For centuries these animals have formed the nucleus of the maritime Eskimo subsistence economy. Such fish as the whitefish, tomcod, salmon trout, and grayling also frequent these waters and are used by the Eskimo, particularly during the summer season.

The Face of the Past

The arctic has served for centuries as a natural laboratory, testing man's ability to survive in a severe environment. Given their specialized way of life, the Eskimo have met this challenge with ingenuity and skill, yet they followed long after the first inhabitants of the far north. Man probably entered the New World by way of an intercontinental land bridge connecting the region of Bering Strait with the Asiatic mainland. We know little of man's antiquity in the northern sector of the Old World, although archeological remains from the Ob River, Lake Baikal, and the upper reaches of the Lena River appear to date as far back as 10,000 to 12,000 years. Conservative estimates place man on the Great Plains and in the southwestern part of the United States more than 15,000 years ago. Sometime prior to this period, man crossed the Bering Strait and drifted east and south. We can only speculate as to why these prehistoric migrations occurred, though it seems reasonable to assume that they were related to alterations in sources and movement of game, climatic changes, and perhaps population pressures. To date no traces of these first Alaskan immigrants have been found.

One of the earliest archeological sites on the Alaskan side of the Bering Strait was excavated in 1948 in the area of Norton Sound immediately south of the Seward Peninsula. Called the Denbigh Flint Complex, this early site has been given a radio-carbon date between 2500 and 3000 B.C. Microlithic tools obtained from the site have definite Old World mesolithic characteristics, which are much older than those of any recognized Eskimo group. These early tools nevertheless appear to be a primary source from which derived another microlithic arctic complex, the well-known Dorset culture.

The Dorset Eskimo, who occupied northern North America from around 700 B.C. to approximately 1200 A.D., left many archeological sites throughout much of the central arctic and as far east as Newfoundland. These people lived in semisubterranean houses with long entrance passages and walls made of heavy stone slabs and boulders. Animal bones found at the site suggest that the Dorset people hunted seal, walrus, polar bear, caribou, rabbit, fox, and birds, but not the whale.

Archeologists also have noted similarities between the Denbigh Flint Complex and the famous Ipiutak site, located near Point Hope, 125 miles north of the Arctic Circle. First inhabited nearly 2000 years ago, this large village of over 600 houses has provided a wealth of information concerning early north Alaskan Eskimo life. There is considerable doubt that all these houses were occupied at any one time, but it does appear that the population of Ipiutak was once considerably larger than that of Point Hope today, perhaps numbering as many as 1500 inhabitants.

The typical Ipiutak house was about twelve to fifteen feet square with sod-covered walls sloping in toward a roof resting on four corner posts. Low benches on three sides of the house were used for sleeping, which left a small floor area, and a shallow depression in the center served as a fireplace. The entrance to the west was followed by a short passage to the main room. There was no low section of the passage to trap cold air and keep it from flowing through the inner door, as has been found in more recent Eskimo dwellings. The bones, tools, weapons, and other equipment found at the site indicate that the Ipiutak Eskimo hunted both land and sea mammals. It is quite probable that these people spent much of the winter inland hunting caribou, returning to the coast in time for the annual walrus migration in the spring, although archeological evidence for this migration pattern is scarce. The Ipiutak Eskimo is considered by many to be somewhat aberrant due to the lack of whale hunting equipment, sleds, harpoon floats, and bow drills, all of which were common to other coastal groups.

These people were outstanding carvers. Some of the elaborate bone and ivory animal carvings and decorations are reminiscent of the scytho-Siberian art, although there is no direct evidence that the ancestors of the Ipiutak people may once have lived in northern Siberia along the Ob and Yenisei rivers.

At the same time people were inhabiting Ipiutak, members of the Old Bering Sea culture occupied other Alaskan Eskimo villages located on Cape Prince of Wales, the Diomede Islands, Saint Lawrence Island, and elsewhere. These Eskimo lived permanently on the coast hunting land and sea mammals. Cultural similarities between these early people and modern residents of the area leave little doubt that continuous development from one to the other has taken place. The earlier Eskimo traveled by kayak and umiak skin boats in summer and hand-drawn sled in winter. Their houses were small semisubterranean dwellings, with the characteristic cold-trap entrance. The long-continued residence of the Old Bering Sea Eskimo in this region is directly related to the great abundance of walrus that inhabit the area. Having resolved many of their subsistence problems, these Eskimo were able to devote increasing amounts of time to the development of technical and artistic skills, for which this group has become so well known.

Sometime after 1000 A.D. some Eskimo spread across the central arctic to Labrador and Greenland. These were the Thule people, a cultural group that originated in Alaska as an outgrowth of the prehistoric Birnick culture of the northwestern Alaskan region. They traveled thousands of miles and built settlements throughout central and eastern Canada and Greenland, and within the past few centuries some of the Thule Eskimo have returned to Alaska. Many traditional elements of Thule culture clearly are present in more recent north Alaskan Eskimo life, including permanent houses of stone, whalebone, and turf, summer conical tents, and soapstone dishes. The Thule Eskimo utilized to the fullest all the natural resources of the arctic, among them, the whale, walrus, seal, bear, caribou, fox, and other small mammals, birds, and fish. Much of the recent north Alaskan technology stems from this earlier Thule culture.

In view of the extreme geographic range over which the Eskimo has lived, it is somewhat surprising to find the modern Eskimo sharing such uniformity of language, physical type, and culture. All Eskimo speak dialects of one linguistic stock, and all are of similar physical type, which suggests that there has been relatively little Indian intrusion into Eskimo territory. Given this over-all similarity, there are nonetheless important regional differences in technology, social structure, and culture. These regional variations in the phrasing of Eskimo life point up rather well one of the dominant values of Eskimo culture, that of flexibility or adaptability.

European Contacts

At the time of the first significant European contact in about 1740, there may have been as many as 40,000 Eskimo living in Alaska. Estimates suggest that over 20,000 lived in the northwest and the interior (Seward Peninsula, arctic slope, and the Brooks Range), with another 12,000 living in the southwest from Bristol Bay to the Yukon delta. In addition, there were thought to be approximately 16,000 Aleut, 11,800 Northwest Coast Indians, and 6900 Athapascan Indians (Swanton 1952).

From the point of view of the Europeans, interest in the Alaskan region can be considered in two phases, each with its specific motives. Russian fur traders, searching for sea otter, fox, and seal pelts, reached the Aleutian Islands in the middle of the eighteenth century. Within a relatively few years disease and senseless murder virtually decimated the native Aleut. Russian traders did not go beyond the Kotzebue Sound and the Eskimo north of this region were not significantly affected by European contact until the middle of the nineteenth century.

The first white explorers to reach north Alaska were Sir John Franklin and Captain F. W. Beechey. These two Englishmen had been sent by the British Admiralty to map the coast west of the Mackenzie River in 1826. Beechey sailed through the Bering Strait toward Point Barrow, while Franklin pressed west along the north coast of Alaska, hoping to meet Beechey coming from the opposite direction. Franklin only reached Return Reef, half way to his destination, but several of Beechey's men did arrive at Point Barrow in August of that year.

Although Franklin and Beechey had relatively little contact with the north Alaskan Eskimo, they both noted the extensive trade carried on by these people with other Eskimo and Indian groups. In his journal Beechey remarked, "The inhabitants of Point Barrow had copper kettles, and were in several respects better supplied with European articles than the people who resided to the southward. . . . The copper kettle in all probability came from the Russians." (Beechey 1832:572)

The explanation for the copper kettles became clear a few years later when John Simpson, a ship's doctor wintering at Point Barrow, learned more about the Eskimo's trading system. His journal tells of four great trade centers. The first at Cape Prince of Wales was a port of entry for Asiatic wares. Here the Siberian Eskimo met the Eskimo from the region of Norton Sound. Once trading at this center had been concluded, the Cape Prince of Wales Eskimo sailed to the second major rendezvous near Kotzebue. At this center, inland Eskimo of the Noatak and Kobuk rivers obtained trade goods of Asiatic origin, which they then took back with them in the fall. The following spring these Eskimo brought goods down the Colville River to the now-abandoned village of Nirlik on the Beaufort Sea, where active commerce took place with the nearby Point Barrow Eskimo. Iron and copper kettles, double-edged knives, tobacco, beads, tin for making pipes, and such items of inland Eskimo manufacture as deer skins, fox fur, feathers for headdresses, and arrows were exchanged for whale and seal oil, whalebone, walrus tusks, sealskin, and other maritime products.

Still later in the summer the Point Barrow Eskimo continued east along the coast to Barter Island, the fourth center, where, with the Mackenzie Eskimo and north Athapascan Indians, they exchanged surplus Russian and inland Eskimo goods for *muktuk* (whale skin), stone lamps, English knives, beads, guns, and ammunition. The English trade goods were obtained from the Mackenzie post of the Hudson's Bay Company. During the following winter some Point Barrow Eskimo regularly sledded to Point Hope where they traded goods previously received from the Mackenzie delta Eskimo.

This important trading system, which had been in existence for many years, was halted with the advent of extensive commercial whaling in the north Bering and Chukchi seas beginning in 1848. Whalers transporting goods chiefly in their own ships and distributing them directly to the Eskimo effectively curtailed the native traders, who could offer little in the way of competition. This, in turn, had a dramatic effect on the inland Eskimo. Many inlanders, no longer able to obtain trade goods upon which they were quite dependent, were forced to move to the coastal villages and learn a new way of life.

Prior to the discovery of the northwest whaling grounds in 1838, this activity was limited to the Atlantic and southern Pacific oceans. Within twelve years of that discovery, whaling ships began to frequent the Arctic Ocean north of the Bering Strait. Based in New England or California, these vessels spent the months from December to March in the waters surrounding the Hawaiian Islands in search of the sperm whale. With the coming of spring they sailed toward the Bering Strait, and beyond, looking for the bowhead. The bowhead whale migrate north toward Point Barrow during the months of May and June. Once past this point they veer east and finally arrive at their summer feeding grounds in the Beaufort Sea. In the fall the ships again followed the whale as they retraced their path along the north Alaskan coast and across the ocean to the western Chukchi Sea.

The whalers were primarily interested in obtaining baleen, the long, thin, flexible strips of keratin (similar in composition to human fingernails) that are found inside the mouth of the bowhead and serve to strain the whale's food from the water. Baleen was used in Europe and the United States for such manufactured products as buttons and corset stays. In the 1850s this material sold for 32¢ a pound, but by the late 1880s, when the hourglass figure had become the prevailing concept of feminine beauty, its value had increased markedly. In 1880 baleen brought $2.00 a pound, and in 1905 it reached a high of almost $5.00 a pound. Since one bowhead could yield a ton of baleen valued at $8000 or more, as well as other marketable products, it is easy to understand why the industry grew so rapidly. During the period from 1895 to 1905 there were fifty-one registered American whalers sailing out of San Francisco, and they produced an annual income of about a million dollars.

By 1867, when Alaska was purchased by the United States, the whalers had become a common sight along the north Alaskan coast, and their crews mingled freely with the local population. Repeating rifles, ammunition, liquor, flour, black tobacoo, matches, lead, and molasses were exchanged in quantity for whalebone, caribou meat, and fur clothing. Although outlawed by the United States government, whiskey was a commonly used trade item, and schooners laden with liquor frequented many coastal villages. As much as $200 worth of furs and other goods might be exchanged for one bottle of whiskey. In the 1880s the steam vessel was introduced into the whaling fleet. Since it was better able to spend the winter in arctic waters, contact between whites and the Eskimo increased proportionately. Whaling and trading stations were set up along the northwestern Alaskan coast and both inland and maritime Eskimo were hired to work as deckhands and guides on ships, or put to work hunting caribou and making fur clothing.

Occasionally ships were caught in new winter ice and destroyed. In 1897 six vessels were trapped off Point Barrow and the 275 marooned men were forced to spend a year on the coast living with the Eskimo. Concerned for their safety, a United States government mercy mission sent 448 reindeer overland to Barrow from herds already located at Teller and farther south. The government had originally obtained the reindeer in 1892 from Siberia in an attempt to establish among the Eskimo a stable economy based on reindeer herding. Since the Barrow Eskimo had been able to provide sufficient food for the marooned men, most of the herd eventually were given to the villagers.

Whaling continued to be such a profitable activity through the early years of the twentieth century that several Eskimo entered into business for themselves. In 1908 the explorer Stefansson found a few Eskimo at Point Barrow maintaining as many as five or six boat crews and paying equal wages with whites. A crew member's earnings of $200 for the six-week whaling season might provide him with sufficient supplies to last throughout the year.

Eventually the whale population began to decline. This decrease, combined with the invention of substitute materials for baleen, and whale oil, brought an end to commercial whaling by 1915. Over the sixty-year period, this industry had dramatically changed Eskimo cultural patterns. With their newly obtained repeating rifles the Eskimo had so reduced the number of land and sea mammals that the old subsistence economy was severely jeopardized. The introduction of whiskey as a trade item had disrupted and demoralized village life. The spread of new diseases such as measles, small pox, and influenza, to which the Eskimo had no immunity, and tuberculosis, took a devastating toll of human life. Some small settlements disappeared entirely. Larger ones like Point Hope lost as much as 12 percent of their population in one year. In 1900, more than 200 inland Eskimo trading at Point Barrow died of influenza following the visit of a whaling ship. Two years later over 100 Barrow Eskimo died in a measles epidemic.

As the plight of the Eskimo became known farther south, pressure to take action was put on the United States government and other organizations. The lack of facilities for education was a cause for concern, and schools were erected in the 1890s at Point Hope, Barrow, and in other villages. Communities like Wainwright were formally recognized only on the construction of a permanent school. With some degree of foresight, Christian churches in Alaska divided their missionary activities into specific territories, and the region north of the Brooks Range was allocated to the Presbyterians. Medical missionaries arrived at Point Barrow and Point Hope in the 1890s. When the school was constructed at Wainwright several years later, this newly formed village was assigned to the Barrow Presbyterian mission.

In an attempt to resolve the problem of depleted game resources, the United States Bureau of Education, which had been given the responsibility for the welfare of the Eskimo, introduced reindeer herding. Reindeer originally purchased from the Siberian Chukchi were brought across the Bering Strait by the Revenue cutters in the 1890s. Herds then were established at schools and church missions throughout western and north Alaska, and Chukchi and Lapp herders were brought to instruct the Eskimo in handling the deer. After he had served an apprenticeship, an Eskimo received the loan of a small herd. Since reindeer multiply rapidly, herdsmen usually were able to repay their loan to the school or mission fairly promptly. Eventually many of these herds grew to phenomenal sizes. The Eskimo herd at Barrow, which began with 125 deer, grew to 30,000 by 1935 (Sonnenfeld 1959). Between 1918 and 1934 the Wainwright herd expanded from 2300 to 22,000.

One reason for this spectacular growth was that the reindeer were introduced into an environment that had been largely cleared of their only possible range competitor, the caribou. Reindeer simply took over the ecological nitch left vacant by the departed caribou. Yet the success of this venture proved only temporary. By 1940, through poor herding, local overgrazing, disease, and predation, the Barrow and other north Alaskan herds were only a fraction of their former sizes. The 1250 deer imported from

Siberia between 1892 and 1902 increased to over 600,000 by 1932; by 1940 only 200,000 head remained, and by 1950 there were less than 25,000.

The causes for these losses were many. The Eskimo's revived interest in hunting as opposed to herding, new employment opportunities, and poor government administration and policies contributed as much to the losses as the more frequently blamed factors such as inadequacies of range, losses to wolves, and the joining of the reindeer with migrating caribou herds.

This, in conjunction with the end of the whaling industry, made life more difficult for the Eskimo. Available reindeer meat reduced the threat of starvation, but land and sea mammals were at a minimum. At the same time, having acquired a desire for Western goods and services, most Eskimo did not wish to return to their traditional subsistence way of life. They needed a cash income to purchase such newly deemed essentials as flour, tobacco, tea, woolen clothing, cloth tents, and iron tools and weapons.

Fortunately, a new source of income became available at this crucial time. Beginning in 1920 fox fur increased steadily in value. The Eskimo had previously supplemented his income with trapping, but it now became his major means of livelihood. White fox pelts sold for as much as $50 and the rarer blue pelts brought more than $100. An annual income of $3000 to $4000 was not unusual and, in rare instances, income reached as high as $7000.

Although the shift from hunting to trapping took place gradually and relatively easily, it had a number of unforeseen consequences for the social and cultural life of the Eskimo. Traditional Eskimo hunting patterns had been based on strong cooperative ties maintained between members of related or quasi-related families. Trapping, in contrast, was a much more individualistic enterprise involving, at most, two related families. Furthermore, it was a winter occupation lasting from November to April—a period previously devoted to extensive community activity, such as informal visiting between friends and relatives, storytelling, and an almost continuous round of entertainment in the Eskimo *karigi* or dance houses. Once having committed themselves to a cash economy based on trapping, the Eskimo frequently spent much of the long dark winter living in lonely driftwood cabins along the coast, far removed from friends and relatives. The consequent reduction of the cooperative bond between kin and enforced winter isolation quickly affected village cohesion.

It would be difficult to determine the extent of the changes that might have occurred if trapping as a major means of livelihood had continued for several generations. Instead, following the depression of 1929, it abruptly became uneconomical. Fox pelts brought such a low price that the Eskimo literally were forced to return to at least a partial subsistence mode of life. Fortunately, seal, walrus, whale, and caribou again had become more plentiful and were hunted regularly. Some semblance of the former community cooperation and solidarity was reinstated, although the village dance houses—viewed critically by the missionaries—had all but disappeared. At this time the Alaskan division of the Bureau of Indian

Affairs (Alaskan Native Service) encouraged the making for sale of such handicrafts as ivory carvings and baskets. Cooperative native stores, organized early in the century by the government to aid the Eskimo to develop greater economic independence and increase his capital, also contributed to the cash income of the shareholders. Although control of the stores tended to fall into the hands of a small number of powerful Eskimo families, often those who had been particularly successful in reindeer herding, the stores did have the effect of tempering the prices of local white traders. Furthermore, the stores provided a local outlet for the Eskimo hunters to sell fresh meat, which was then sold to other Eskimo engaged in nonhunting activities.

Other sources of cash income became available in the middle and late 1930s when Old Age Pensions, general relief, Aid for Dependent Children allotments, and other government subsidies were given to the Eskimo. Post offices, located in every community with a school, provided salary for an Eskimo postmaster, and wages usually were paid to school janitors, native-store employees, and mission helpers. Nevertheless, until the end of World War II the economy of north Alaska was both unstable and unpredictable. General health was so poor that half the young Eskimo men who volunteered for military duty had to be discharged as physically unfit. Ten percent of all Eskimo children died before their first birthday. Ninety percent of Alaska's deaths from tuberculosis occurred among the Eskimo (Alaska Health Survey Team 1954:32).

Following the end of World War II, new economic opportunities became available to the north Alaskan Eskimo. In 1946, the United States Navy sponsored the search for petroleum in the regions north of the Brooks Range and set up a large construction camp a few miles from Barrow village. Eskimo were encouraged to find employment at the camp, and many of those who could pass the physical examination found that they could earn salaries as high as $6000 per year. So many jobs were available that some Eskimo moved to Barrow from villages as far away as Point Hope and Aklavik in Canada. At the same time the United States Coast and Geodetic Survey began extensive mapping of the northern coast, and jobs as surveying assistants and guides gave employment to other Eskimo.

Perhaps the greatest over-all change in recent years has been the result of the construction of the Distant Early Warning (DEW) Line radar installations. These sites, stretching across the whole of the North American arctic were built in the years between 1953 and 1957. Many of the north Alaskan Eskimo hired as construction workers on these sites still are employed as maintenance and repair men. In 1962, over half of the Eskimo men at Kaktovik were earning salaries of $600 or more a month at the Barter Island site. At Point Barrow they are hired by the military, the Federal Aviation Agency, the Weather Bureau, and other government organizations maintaining bases or stations in the area.

Although an increasing number of north Alaskan Eskimo are becoming relatively affluent, some still rely on hunting and fishing to supply most of their daily needs. The Eskimo of today is living in two worlds and he is not always sure which of the two he prefers. He knows well that the period of economic plenty he now is enjoying may soon disappear, as have all similar periods. Still, he feels that he should take advantage of the improved facilities for health and education that are offered to him, learn more about the outside world, and prepare his children to live with or in it. The problems are those of transitional people everywhere. The answers sought by the Eskimo reflect their previous way of life and their general outlook on the world. How they go about solving these problems will be our major concern in the rest of this book.

2

Growing Up

Attitudes toward Children

CHILDREN are a dominant feature of all north Alaskan Eskimo communitities, both in number and in respect to the attention given them by their elders. The Eskimo child is considered a vital part of the family and enjoys much love and affection, from both parents. Eskimo men are gentler and more demonstrative than are fathers in Western society. Since they greatly value large families, most families range in size from seven to twelve, depending on the number of children that survive the early illnesses and diseases. Birth control seldom is practiced, and only the mothers who have begun to adopt Western values express any interest in limiting their families.

Rarely is there strong preference for one sex or the other. Some families want the first-born to be a girl who can help care for those that follow; others want a boy because he can soon contribute to the family's subsistence needs. No matter what the parents' preference is, a baby of either sex is welcomed on arrival with great affection.

Sometimes a family has more children than it wants or can adequately support. When this happens, an infant may be "offered" to another family. This form of adoption has a long history among the Eskimo and is still prevalent. A child also may be adopted because the foster parents are childless, because his own parents have died, or because he is illegitimate and can be given a better upbringing in a home with a father. (Except in the more acculturated sectors of the community, illegitimacy does not carry the stigma it does in Western society.) Also, for various reasons a child may live for a long time with relatives, a custom which clearly strengthens the traditional extended family ties.

Adoption is usually, though not necessarily, arranged between kin; in recent years some Eskimo infants have been given to northern white families. An adopted child always uses the terms "father" and "mother" to his foster parents even when he is closely related to them. The child's origin never is concealed and in many instances he is considered as belonging to both families. He may call the two sets of parents by the same names and maintain strong bonds with his real parents and siblings. In undertaking genealogical studies, anthropologists often have become confused about the biological parents of an adopted child since both sets claim him. It is evident that, whatever the reasons for adoption, the parents usually treat a foster child with as much warmth and affection as they do their own.

Birth and Infancy

Traditionally there were many taboos relating to pregnancy, which if broken, might result in harm to mother or child. For example, a pregnant woman who walked backward out of a house might have a breech delivery. Putting a pot over her head could cause a mother to be unable to deliver the placenta, and sleeping at odd hours might give her a lazy child. Today most Eskimo women laugh at these beliefs, but a few, particularly older ones, still adhere to them.

In the past a birth took place in a special parturition lodge, known as the *aanigutyak*. In winter, it was a snowhouse built for the purpose by the father, and the woman entered it as soon as she began labor. She gave birth in a kneeling position with the help of an assistant, who usually was a female relative with some experience in delivering babies. Today women without access to the public health hospital at Barrow have their children at home helped by specially trained midwives, of which there are six at Point Hope. Barter Island and Wainwright women are likely to go to the Barrow hospital.

Many stories have circulated in the north about the hardiness of the Eskimo woman giving birth under very difficult circumstances, and there is little doubt that many of these stories are true. VanStone (1962:79) speaks of the woman traveling by boat to Point Hope who asked to be put ashore "to go to the toilet." She gave birth after the boat had moved on without her, cut the cord, and scraped sand over the afterbirth. Putting the child in her parka, she ran along the beach to catch up with the boat.

Before a child is a month old he is customarily baptized by the church and given a name. Today every child receives an English name and at least one Eskimo name. These names, usually given by the parents, are often those of recently deceased relatives or highly respected individuals. When English names were introduced early in the century, the traditional Eskimo ones were used as family names.

According to the old convictions, the name given to the child carried with it the qualities of the individual from whom the name was taken. When an older living person's name was used, he would often give gifts to the child. This action was prompted by the belief that after his death the donor's spirit would survive in the namesake. Although they are sensitive to the skeptical attitude of whites, many Eskimo still carry at least a vestige of this concept.

When a baby is two or three months old the mother begins to pass some of the responsibility for his care to older siblings and her unmarried sisters and cousins. In these circumstances a child soon becomes accustomed to having a variety of tenders and the pattern continues until he can care for himself.

From birth a baby is packed, or carried in the back of a parka, by his mother or other female relatives. If the mother is busy and no one else is available to carry him, she may put him in a crib to play or sleep. If he cries, she soon picks him up and plays with him. Occasionally an acculturated mother complains that her baby wants to be held too much and is "spoiled," but seldom does any Eskimo woman completely disregard her child's cries.

The mother customarily packs her baby until he is two years old, or until another child is born. Strapped in place by a belt that goes around the mother's waist and under his buttocks, he has little freedom of movement. He does have occasion to learn to walk, though, and can usually get about quite well by the time he is two. Sometimes a child over that age asks to be carried, and although the mother may fulfill his wish, siblings and friends are likely to tease him good-naturedly.

The Eskimo infant rarely has a set feeding or sleeping schedule, which hardly is surprising considering the lack of schedule of most Eskimo adults. When the baby cries it is fed, whether by breast or bottle. In recent years bottle feeding has become increasingly common among those families who have sufficient cash income to obtain canned milk. By the age of one, the child eats solid foods including homemade broths and premasticated meat. Weaning is a gradual process and may not be completed until the third or even the fourth year. An older child rarely is rejected in favor of a younger one, and the transition appears to be very easy.

Toilet training, in contrast, is begun early, usually before the first birthday. The mother holds the child on a pot on her lap blowing gently on his head. When the desired result has been obtained, she indicates her pleasure with a few kind words and playful movements.

The soft caribou skin and moss used by earlier north Alaskan Eskimo now have been replaced by cloth diapers, and as a baby grows older, he is given "training pants," castoff clothing open at the crotch. Accidents and near misses are treated very lightly, although they may bring some gentle rebuke. Even chronic bed-wetters are not punished, except among Westernized families, where the offender is made to stay in bed longer than usual.

In general, there is no aura of shame or secrecy about excretory functions, and no reticence about discussing them. During the course of fieldwork, one anthropologist was given a vivid description of the effects of eating *ugrook* meat on the bowels. Children may say to one another "don't look," but girls under four and all boys urinate unconcernedly anywhere out of doors.

Given the combination of large families and small houses, Eskimo sleeping arrangements vary markedly from Western patterns. Formerly, infants slept with their parents; today, the youngest sleep in cribs, the next oldest child or children with their parents, and still older ones with each other. As many as four siblings of different sexes may sleep in the same bed, all wrapped in one blanket. A youth is given a separate bed on reaching adolescence, and if the size of the room permits, he may have a cubbyhole or corner of the room to himself. If the house is small and crowded, however, quite grown-up children sleep with the parents. Only in the most Westernized, well-to-do family does each child have a bed of his own.

Discipline seldom is imposed on the child before he is one year old. This is of little significance since a child packed on his mother's back most of the time offers few problems. Only when he has sufficient freedom of movement to *pakak*,—get into things he should not—is he checked.

Concepts of hygiene vary widely and appear to be in direct proportion to the degree of Westernization. Only the more acculturated mother will express concern about her baby's putting a dirty object from the floor to his mouth, or will not pass a bottle from a sick child to a well one. In short, infant care consists primarily of keeping the baby happy; for the baby this means being held, cuddled, fed, rested, warmed, and kept dry.

Childhood

"How have the Eskimo managed to raise their children so well?" The woman asking the question recently had become a teacher in a large north Alaskan village. She spoke warmly of her pupils' good humor, liveliness, resourcefulness, and well-behaved manner. Although she later learned that Eskimo children have their difficulties and conflicts, that they can be fretful, cruel, and petulant, her first impressions had merit. Patient and obedient, yet outgoing and enthusiastic, these young people are quick to offer help when it is needed. They do indeed exemplify qualities that many Western parents would like to see manifest in their own children. To rephrase the teacher's question, what are the experiences of Eskimo upbringing that favor the development of these attributes?

Certainly, the warmth and affection given infants by parents, siblings, and other relatives provide them with a deep feeling of well-being and security. Young children also feel important because they learn early that they are expected to be useful, working members of the family. This attitude is not instilled by imposing tedious chores, but rather by including children in the round of daily activities, which enhances the feeling of family participation and cohesion. To put it another way, parents rarely deny children their company or exclude them from the adult world.

This pattern reflects the parents' views of child rearing. Adults feel that they have more experience in living and it is their responsibility to share this experience with the children, "to tell them how to live." Children have to be told repeatedly because they tend to forget. Misbehavior is due to a child's forgetfulness, or to improper teaching in the first place. There is rarely any thought that the child is basically nasty, willful, or sinful. Where Anglo-Americans applaud a child for his good behavior, the Eskimo praise him for remembering.

One can see examples of this attitude in many situations. A father once was observed lecturing in Eskimo to his children before they set out on a short camping trip. Asked to expand on his remarks, he said:

We stir them up a little to live right. Tell them to obey the parents. Do what people tell them to do. And like now, when they go on a camping trip, not to take a new pillow. It get dirty on the trip. Take old one. They young. They don't know what to do. We tell them how to do things. Like our parents used to tell us. Same they used to talk to us. We used to talk a lot like that but we haven't lately. We begin again. Stir them up. They forget.

Another man discussed his nephew's helpless panic during a hunting trip when a severe storm had threatened to wipe out the camp. Waking at night to find the tent blowing away and their boat temporarily lost, the boy had become frozen with fear. Never suggesting that he was cowardly or weak, the man was critical of the lad's behavior, but explained it in terms of his not having had sufficient camping experience to know what to do.

Fathers participate almost as much as do mothers in modern family life, and in disciplinary matters they appear to fulfill much the same function that they do in Western society. A mother may say to a recalcitrant child, "Wait till I tell your father!" or "Wait till your father comes home. You gonna get a licking!" In the less acculturated families, the father retains the dominant, rather than equal-participant, role. In these homes a child is expected to be restrained, quiet, and respectful in his father's presence.

Regardless of the degree of Westernization, more emphasis is placed on equality than on superordination-subordination in parent-child relations. A five year old obeys, not just because he fears punishment or loss of love, but because he identifies with his parents and respects their judgment. Thus he finds little to resist or rebel against in his dealings with adults. We will find rebellion more common in adolescents, but it is not necessarily a revolt against parental control.

By the time a child reaches the age of four or five, his parents' initial demonstrativeness has become tempered with an increased interest in his activities and accomplishments. They watch his play with obvious pleasure, respond warmly to his conversation, make jokes with him, and discipline him.

Though a child is given considerable autonomy and his whims and wishes are treated with respect, he is nonetheless taught to obey all adults. To an outsider unfamiliar with parent-child relations, the tone of Eskimo commands and admonitions sometimes sounds harsh and angry, yet in few instances does a child respond as if he had been addressed hostilely.

A youngster who whines, sulks, cries, or expresses some other unacceptable emotion is told flatly, "Be nice!" If he appears to be getting into mischief he is warned, "Don't *pakak!*" There are other frequently heard admonitions. "Don't *ipagak!*" means do not play in the water or on the beach; "Shut the door," protects against the cold; "Put your parka on," guarantees adequate dress for the out of doors; "Don't go in someone else's house when there is no one at home," reflects concern for others' property. Perhaps most common is "Don't fight!" which is directed not only against personal assaults and rock throwing, but also against verbal quarrels.

There are certain acts, like "taking without asking," and those involving potential dangers, that do lead to punishment. If admonitions are unsuccessful, threats of such fearsome creatures as *inyakuns* (little people), *nanooks* (bears), and *tanniks* (white men) are brought in for support. Or, the threat may be unspecified, as in "Somebody out there, somebody gonna get you."

If this does not have an effect, the misbehaving child is dealt with more severely. The adult may shout, threaten, or actually strike the child, although physical punishment is relatively rare. The child may be isolated, a form of punishment reserved for more serious breaches like fighting or playing with water in below-freezing temperatures. In line with the attitude that children are ignorant and forgetful, punishment is accompanied by explanation and reasoning. Seldom is anything more than mild humiliation or teasing used as a negative sanction.

A child's reaction to any of these treatments may range from compliance, temporary tears, or unhappy looks—both of which are ignored—to sulking, rebellious shrieks, or silent resistance. This latter takes the form of ignoring the orders or repeating the behavior to see if the adult will take notice. It is rare indeed to hear a child talk back, verbally refuse to perform the action, or say petulantly, "I don't want to." Sometimes a child does threaten vengeance—when he is angry at another child or an outsider, such as a *tannik*—but it is most unusual to hear threats directed at parents or adult relatives. By adolescence discipline seems to consist entirely of lectures, although they still may be delivered in the harsh tone that characterizes Eskimo cautions.

After the age of five a child is less restricted in his activities in and around the village, although theoretically he is not allowed on the beach or ice without an adult. During the dark winter season, he remains indoors or stays close to the house to prevent him from getting lost and to protect him from polar bears which might come into the village. In summer, though, children play at all hours of the day or "night" or as long as their parents are up.

By the eighth year some of the responsibility for a child's socialization has been passed on from adults to his peers. Children frequently tell each other the same things adults tell them: "Don't fight," "Don't *pakak*," "You supposed to knock," "Shut the door." Rule breaking usually is reported to the nearest adult: "Mom, Sammy *ipagak*." Tattling is not deprecated to the extent that it was traditionally (Spencer 1959:240). Furthermore, not only older children "play parent" and try to impose adult rulings on younger ones; all children instruct all others, no matter what their ages are. Such instruction generally is taken in good spirit; when an older child reminds a younger one, "You supposed to knock," he is likely to smile sheepishly, go out of the room, knock, and enter again.

Although not burdened with responsibility, both boys and girls are expected to take an active role in family chores. In the early years responsibilities are shared, depending on who is available. Regardless of sex, it is important for a child to know how to perform a wide variety of tasks and give help when needed. Both sexes collect and chop wood, get water, help carry meat and other supplies, oversee younger siblings, run errands for adults, feed the dogs, and burn trash.

As a child grows older, more specific responsibilities are allocated to him, according to his sex. Boys as young as seven may be given an opportunity to shoot a .22 rifle, and at least a few boys in every village have killed their first caribou by the time they are ten. A youngster learns techniques of butchering while on hunting trips with older siblings and adults, although he is seldom proficient until he is in his mid-teens. In the past girls learned butchering at an early age, since this knowledge was essential to attracting a good husband. Today, with the availability of large quantities of Western foods, this skill may not be acquired until a girl is married, and not always then.

Although there is a recognized division of labor by sex, it is far from rigid at any age level. Boys, and even men, occasionally sweep the house and cook. Girls and their mothers go on fishing or bird-hunting trips. Members of each sex can usually assume the responsibilities of the other when the need arises, albeit in an auxiliary capacity.

Siblings play together more happily than do most brothers and sisters in Western society, but sibling rivalry and hostility are not completely absent. Hostility often is demonstrated by tattling or engaging in some form of physical abuse. Verbal abuse rarely is expressed. Although tattling is, for the most part, an acceptable form of aggression, physical abuse is not. Anyone who indulges in hard pushing, elbowing, pinching, or hitting is told immediately to stop. Rather than fight back, the injured party usually requests help from an older sibling or nearby adult.

Competitiveness, indirectly expressed, characterizes many of the children's activities. In games involving athletic prowess a child says, "Look how far I can throw the stone," rather than "I can throw the stone farther than you." When rivalry is open, it is expected that the game be undertaken in good spirit and the skills of one participant not flaunted at the expense of the other's feelings. Aggressive competitiveness always is condemned, as when a father chides his son, "Why you always wanting to win?"

Only very young children play regularly with others of like age. As they reach five or six, the age range of their playmates widens considerably. Team games or those, such as Norwegian ball, involving many people, may have as participants children of both sexes between five and twelve years old. It is not until adolescence that a young person actively sets himself apart from other children. Youth of this age group may briefly watch youngsters play volleyball or some other game, but they seldom participate. Adults encourage this separation, and, when they see a teen-age boy or girl playing with younger children, they may say, "That person is a little slow in his development."

There are a great many games that Eskimo children play regularly. Some involving feats of skill and strength, formalized wrestling, and hand games have a long history among the Eskimo. Others, such as kick-the-can, London Bridge, volleyball, soccer, Annie-over, and, more recently, Monopoly and Scrabble, are of Western origin. Still other games combine elements of both. *Haku,* an Eskimo team game in which the object is to make the members of the opposite team laugh, includes amusing portrayals of Hawaiian and Spanish dances done, if possible, with a straight face. A few traditional Eskimo games like *putigarok,* a form of tag where the person who is "it" must touch another on the same spot on the body on which he was tagged, closely resemble Western forms of tag. Kaktovik children occasionally play a fantasy game called "polar bear" in which one child takes the role of an old woman who falls asleep. A polar bear then comes and takes away her child. She wakes and attempts to discover where the bear has hidden the child. At Barrow village, Eskimo children once played a slightly different version of the same game, called "old woman." A child played the role of an old woman who pretended to be blind; when some of her possessions were stolen, she "accused" other children of taking them. This type of game requires a fair amount of verbal exchange, and the more able talker is the winner.

Storytelling is one of the most popular forms of Eskimo entertainment, especially during the winter months when there is little outside activity. Typical stories contain autobiographical or biographical accounts of unusual incidents, accidents, hunting trips, or other events deemed interesting to the listener. Following the evening meal, a father may call the children around him and recount his last whale hunt, or tell how he shot his first polar bear. A good storyteller acts out part of the tale, demonstrating how he threw the harpoon at the whale's back, or how the bear scooped up the lead dog and sent him flying across the ice. Other stories told by older people describe life long ago before many *tannik*s arrived. Myths and folk tales often portray the exploits of northern animals and birds endowed with supernatural qualities.

Children, too, like to tell stories to each other. These short stories, usually describe some recent activity, real or imagined. Many young Eskimo are passionately fond of horror stories, and a vivid description of raw heads and bloody bones immediately elicits delighted screams of fear from the throats of the listeners. If the teller acts out part of the story, so much the better.

The Eskimo child's creative imagination is reflected in all the activities of telling stories, imitating others, playing store, and inventing new games. Young girls turn a bolt of cloth into a regal gown which they wear to an imaginary ball. Boys of four climb under a worn blanket with their make-believe airplanes to practice night flying. Charging over the tundra with sharply pointed sticks, a pair of six year olds hunt their supposed furry opponent.

This kind of spontaneity, supported by flexible routines and a minimum of rules, obtains until the early teens when events of the real world begin to offer greater challenge. Only in the confines of the classroom do these children find their emotional freedom curtailed.

All Eskimo children from six to sixteen are required to attend the Bureau of Indian Affairs (BIA) school. Parents generally agree that school is a necessary part of the modern child's education, and children themselves usually enjoy the contrast of school and home life. Still, the aims of school differ markedly from those of everyday Eskimo life, and many a child would prefer lessons in hunting to those in arithmetic, geography, social studies, and English. The BIA teacher soon learns that "Work first and play later," "Keep clean," "Don't use your fingers when you eat," and "Remember the time" are all Western admonitions that have little meaning in the child's home life.

The school term in most north Alaskan villages begins in August and continues for 180 days, the number required by the government. Acknowledging the limitations placed on the student's behavior during that period, it is still possible to summarize Eskimo childhood as a time of relative freedom and independence. Participation in simple household tasks still permits boys and girls large amounts of free time. As they grow older they gradually assume the more adult responsibilities of hunting, caring for younger siblings, preparing of food, and cleaning house, but, apart from the school experience, there is at no time a sharp break in the continuity of learning between infancy, childhood, and early adolescence.

There is even greater continuity in child raising today than in the past. In an earlier period changes in clothing delineated the transition from childhood to adolescence. When a boy's voice began to change, he was given a different style of short trousers. Sometime later, when his father or male guardian decided that he was ready for marriage, a minor operation was performed by cutting two slits at the corners of his mouth. After the wounds were cleansed decorative labrets were placed in the openings, thereby signifying that the boy had become a man and was ready for marriage.

A girl's transition to adolescence came with her first menstruation, at which time she was placed in temporary isolation. As she further matured, marked by the growth of her breasts, she exchanged the clothes of childhood for those of adult women. At this stage many women were traditionally tattooed, the mark consisting of a series of closely drawn parallel lines extending from the center of the lower lip to the chin. A few women of sixty-five or more still carry these symbols of early womanhood. Today, however, these customs marking differences in age and sex are all obsolete.

Youth and Courtship

Much of Eskimo child rearing is designed to prepare the young person to assume the orientations and values of the adult group. He is made to feel that his contributions and participation are important to the life of the family. He is taught many of the basic techniques of subsistence and responsibilities of the home, and he learns the cultural traditions that he is expected to follow as an adult. In spite of this background, and in part because of it, many adolescents feel unprepared to assume the responsibilities of modern adult life and, as a result, they are in general the least well-adjusted of any age group.

Because of the rapid changes that are occurring all around them, they no longer have a clear picture of the adult role. Taught from childhood that an Eskimo should be self-reliant and a good hunter, a boy finds his father seeking salaried employment at a government or military installation and hunting only on week ends or during vacations. A girl observes her mother's confusion as she tries to understand the educational, social, and economic changes that are going on within and outside her home. In some respects the problems of the wives and mothers are greater than those of the men, since most adult Eskimo women have much less contact with the Western world, and thus less awareness of the nature of the changes that are occurring.

In school the pupil comes to realize that the Eskimo are a small and relatively unimportant segment of the world's population, and that much of what transpires in national and international affairs passes them by without consideration. This is in sharp contrast to the traditional Eskimo's view of himself, and it does not enhance his sense of self-respect and worth.

Although the village school informs him of the outside world, it hardly prepares him to live with or in it. He learns to speak English, and if he completes elementary school he can read and write. To enter a technical high school he must leave his community for several years and travel to Sitka, Anchorage, or some other town or city about which he knows little. If he chooses not to continue school, and the choice is often left to the youth himself, he soon learns that his lack of skills places him at a disadvantage when competing with whites for northern jobs. If he decides, consciously or unconsciously, to identify with whites by assuming their manner of dress, hair style, and speech, he may find himself criticized for exaggerating their behavior by the very people he is emulating.

Thus, the youth is in many respects "trapped" by his culture. He has little incentive to follow the ways of the past and few skills that enable him to plan for the future. It is hardly surprising, therefore, that most Eskimo adolescents devote their time and energy to matters of the present.

The problem is compounded by the freedom given the youth by his parents and other relatives. We have noted that Eskimo childhood becomes more peer centered with increasing age and that older siblings take on much of the responsibility for socialization of the younger ones. By the time the child reaches adolescence, most of his time is spent with others of his approximate age. This traditional pattern still is given strong support by contemporary Eskimo parents. Most parents have limited knowledge or understanding of their adolescent children's thoughts and behavior. When pressed to discuss a son's or daughter's plans for continuing school, a father is likely to reply, "I don't know. He hasn't told us yet." This lack of communication between parents and youth, coming at a time when the latter are searching for new models of behavior, does little to resolve their feelings of insecurity and isolation.

In these circumstances, Eskimo teen-agers derive their strongest emotional ties from one another, and in many respects seem to form a closed social group. They spend most of their time together and have similar, mostly Western, styles of dress, slang expressions, and mannerisms. Clothing styles, particularly, are like those of their counterparts to the south. The only Eskimo clothing regularly worn by the youth are the fur parkas, and, less regularly, kamik boots. Boys wear slacks of denim or wool, sport shirts and sweaters, shoepacks and rubber boots, and even black leather jackets with names emblazoned on the back. Girls like slacks or wool skirts, slips, brassieres, sweaters, and wool jackets or coats. For parties they enjoy wearing nylon stockings, dresses, and high-heeled shoes. Jewelry and cosmetics, and sometimes even a home permanent, complete the picture.

The girls devote a great deal of attention to their clothes. They work and rework them, changing a hem here, fixing a cuff there, polishing, and cleaning. Some may change their attire several times a day, and, in contrast to married women and children, almost all dress up for evening church services or other events at which boys may be present.

Teen-age slang is strikingly Western in origin. "Man, I don't go for parkas," "Crazy, man," "Yeah, hey," and similar expressions have startled many whites, including the author, on their first visit to a north Alaskan Eskimo village. Recent dance steps and popular songs are learned promptly from radio, movies, teen-age magazines, white friends, individuals who have taken trips to urban centers in the south, and recently returned hospital patients.

Schools have been a part of north Alaskan community life since the late 1800s, although in some isolated villages like Kaktovik and Anaktuvuk Pass, they are of much more recent origin. Teachers, too, are an important source of Western influence: spoken Eskimo is discouraged, if not forbidden, in the classroom; schoolbooks are primarily the standard texts used in the south; and the subjects of hygiene, cleanliness, and manners receive much attention, all of which emphasizes the Western point of view.

In the early 1950s the United States Public Health Service undertook an intensive campaign to decrease the spread of tuberculosis in Alaska. As part of this plan, many north Alaskan Eskimo young people were sent out to sanitariums in Alaska, and as far south as the state of Washington. (Others, still living in the village, are placed on a chemotherapy program in an attempt to arrest their illness.) More than twelve of the fifty Kaktovik adolescents have spent between nine months and two years in these sanitariums, and more will go in the future. Children and adults from Barrow, Wainwright, and Point Hope also have been to these hospitals. Although the effect of hospital life on a youth depends largely on his age, the severity of his illness, and the length of stay, all patients return with a greater awareness of the outside world and they pass on this awareness to others. Some very young children come back no longer able to speak Eskimo; some older ones no longer want to.

In addition to school and hospital experiences, travel implements the spread of Western ideas. Each year youths take trips from their villages to Fairbanks, Anchorage, and farther south to visit friends and relatives who have migrated to these urban centers. When they come home, their less experienced peers are an avid audience for stories of their travels.

Barrow itself is a major center of Western influence, particularly for residents of nearby villages like Wainwright. The extensive medical, educational, and other United States government facilities found at Barrow, and the various religious missionary groups based there, enable the Eskimo and whites to be in closer contact than they can be in other north Alaskan communities. The effect of this social and economic contact reaches all levels of Barrow society, including the teen-agers, and their degree of Western sophistication serves as an influential model for their friends in other villages.

Finally, newspapers, mail-order catalogues, teen-age magazines, religious tracts, comics, radios, records, tape recordings, and even an occasional *TV Guide* find their way into many Eskimo homes and are thoroughly absorbed by the young. Movies, whether obtained from mail-order houses, nearby military sites, or religious groups, are immensely popular. Barrow has its own movie theater which shows commercial films several times a week.

The strong emotional bonds formed between teen-agers, in combination with their active interest in the outside world, tend to drive a wedge between them and their parents. Seldom do Eskimo youths voluntarily engage in activities, other than those associated with household chores or hunting, with their parents and older relatives. By fourteen they have won privileges younger children do not have; in particular, they may smoke, play cards, and stay up at night as long as they like. They also have greater freedom in making their own decisions, although the rest of the household may suffer resulting hardship. Youths who wish to attend private schools, such as Sheldon Jackson Junior College in Sitka, Alaska, are indulged, even when the family's income cannot comfortably cover the $500 tuition.

In addition, following the traditional custom, parents and older relatives refuse to interpret their young people's actions, just as they refuse to account for those of other adults. A parent, asked what his child planned to do upon completion of junior college, answered, "I don't know," even though it was common knowledge that the student planned to teach school.

Because the teen-ager identifies more with Western ideas and concepts than with traditional ones, and is as yet unable to assume full adult responsibilities, he often finds himself with little to do and is, as a result, bored. One hears complaints of restlessness: "There is nothing to do," or "The day goes so slowly at home." The restless feeling differs qualitatively among individuals. Adolescents in isolated villages wish for the more active life at Barrow; some Barrow youths say they are bored because they do not have sufficient access to Western movies, dancing, parties, and other activities. A few of the girls reject Eskimo boys as potential marriage partners and wish more *tannik* men were available; at Kaktovik, where Air Force personnel once lived adjacent to the village, some of the girls wished for the days ". . . when we used to have lots of white boy friends, have lots of fun, and go for walks together." The more dissatisfied say, "I think I will go to Barrow. There, they have movies all the time and the streets are full of people."

Some are discontented with village life for entirely different reasons: they feel left behind in the sweep of new trends. These youths are older, have had less schooling, and have never lived or visited outside the village. They sit on the side lines at parties or dances and say wistfully, "Gee, I feel lonely," or "I wish they would play games I know how to play." Though they are less strongly identified with the Western world, they are not traditionalists either. Trying to bridge the two worlds, they find few friends outside their own group.

When not occupied with school or home responsibilities, most teenagers spend their time together, visiting, playing cards, singing, or going for walks. Group singing, often with guitar accompaniment, is particularly popular, and eight or ten young people often remain after an evening church service to sing hymns and popular songs. Then they may go for a walk, or join others at one of the local coffee shops. Dances and parties are scheduled several times a year at the National Guard Armory or some other community building. Movies always are well patronized when available, and in summer organized ball games attract many participants and spectators. Very recently, making tapes has become a recreation; a group records songs, news, and stories to be mailed to friends and relatives in other villages, who in turn record and send on their taped "letters."

The traditional teen-age pastimes of hunting, fishing, camping, and boating still offer strong appeal. Groups of boys and girls go on all-day outings. If they learn that a young couple is camping along the coast, they may visit the couple over night or for a longer period. Young married couples staying at fish camps during the summer are seldom free of visitors for very long.

Teen-agers consider staying up all night an entertainment in itself. When deciding how to spend an evening, they respond to the suggestion, "Let's stay up," in the same manner that they do "Let's make a tape," or "Let's go for a walk."

Boys and girls in their early teens rarely pair off. Most social contacts are sought with the group rather than with individuals. They may tease each other with "You interested in him, right?" but it is not until the age of fifteen or sixteen that a young person develops a strong interest in members of the opposite sex. At this time a boy may begin to pay particular attention to a girl, talk more with her than with others, sit beside her in church, and in other ways let her know of his interest. Except in the more sophisticated segment of Barrow teen-age life, physical demonstrativeness in front of others is deemed improper. Even at Barrow, putting an arm around a girl's shoulder or giving her a squeeze is usually done in a joking manner, for any open evidence of affection embarrasses both the girl and her friends.

Boys rarely visit girls in their homes unless older family members are there, and it is even less common for a girl to visit a boy's home. But as a youth becomes older he attempts to arrange clandestine meetings by passing a note at school or church to suggest a time and place. Usual meeting places are in homes of young married couples, or, during summer, along the shore or inland.

By the middle teens, girls are very much aware of the boys' attentions. Their conversations center around boys and their activities, and they dress for boys, giggle about them, and show each other pictures of their favorite boy friends.

The late teens brings more sexual experimentation. Some boys have had intercourse by the age of sixteen, and most have by their early twenties. Girls do not usually solicit this degree of involvement, but once started they seem to be unable to avoid further episodes. Finding a secluded meeting place presents problems, particularly in winter. Homes of young married couples are often available, but privacy is limited.

Parents may express among themselves some concern about their children's activities in this area, but they seldom voice these feelings openly or directly. Church precepts do not condone premarital sex, but this has, as yet, had little effect on behavior. Aboriginally, the Eskimo imposed no clearly defined restrictions. At infancy, children became aware of others engaging in intercourse. Masturbation was not forbidden. At the time of puberty, boys and girls occasionally traveled together away from the village, and they often contracted a quasi-married relationship, which might or might not become permanent. Too, men might undertake several trial marriages before choosing one or more wives. Unbridled promiscuity, however, never was sanctioned in the past, nor is it sanctioned today.

In summary, today's young Eskimo face a difficult future for which they have few skills. On the surface they exhibit a markedly Western veneer; underneath they are very unsure of themselves and what they want

to become. Few plan realistically for the future. Some speak of going away to school to become trained in professional or semiprofessional work related to education, welfare, or nursing. Others want to become skilled construction workers, bookkeepers, cooks, or scientists. Making money is in itself an accepted goal of many youth regardless of the kind of position it entails, and there is an unrealistic assumption that jobs will be available whenever needed. Significantly, most young people want to remain in north Alaska; even those who go away to school plan to return. If those few now in advanced technical and academic training do return to their communities, they will be helpful indeed in guiding other youths to follow similar paths. Well-trained young people taking positions of leadership and responsibility in their own communities will contribute more than any other single factor to ensuring a satisfactory future for the north Alaskan Eskimo.

3

Making a Living

The Seasonal Round

I N NORTH ALASKA, barren land and severe climate continually test the Eskimo's ingenuity and skill at making a living. The Eskimo are closely bound to their natural environment and must adapt to its seasonal variations, though less today then in the past. Even recent immigrants to the far north, whose advanced technology enables them to erect an artificial environment within which they spend most of their time, are only partially insulated from the external world around them. Actually these newcomers rely so heavily on their artificially constructed surroundings that, when their technology fails them, they are unable to cope with arctic conditions.

The Eskimo, in contrast, have less control over their environment and are thus more dependent upon it. Increased opportunities for cash income are not universal and many Eskimo still spend much of their time in the traditional economic pursuits of hunting and fishing. Since these activities are seasonal in nature, the subsistence cycle of the modern Eskimo is very like that which obtained in the past.

The traditional calendar of the north Alaskan Eskimo (Milan 1958: 17–18) illustrates the significance of the changing seasons to their economic and social life:

North Alaskan Aboriginal Calendar

JANUARY
siqinaicaq taatqiq   "the moon of the coming sun"
izraaciaq taatqiq   "the cold moon"

FEBRUARY
siginaasurgruk taatqiq   "the moon with a higher sun"
izraasugruk taatqiq   "the coldest moon"

MARCH
paniksiqsiivik taatqiq "the moon for hanging up seal and caribou skins to bleach them"

APRIL
agaviksiuuvik taatqiq "the moon for beginning whaling"
gurigiiliguvik taatqiq "the moon for finding ptarmigan"

MAY
irniivik taatqiq "the moon when birds and fawns are born"
qauqirivik taatqiq "the moon when eider ducks have returned to the north"

JUNE
supplauavik taatqiq "the moon when rivers commence to flow"

JULY
innauguvik taatqiq "the moon when birds are being formed in eggs"

AUGUST (included in July or September)

SEPTEMBER
tinniuvik taatqiq "the moon when young geese and brant fly south"

OCTOBER
nuliaavik taatqiq "the moon when caribou rut"

NOVEMBER
uvluilaq taatqiq "the moon of the short day"

DECEMBER
siqinrilaq taatqiq "the moon with no sun"

Spring marks the beginning of the whaling season along the coast from Point Hope to Barrow. From early April through June, village boat crews encamp on the edge of the sea ice to hunt the migrating bowhead. These mammals, weighing up to fifty tons, yield enormous quantities of meat and blubber. When a bowhead is brought in, all available members of the community gather to help with the butchering. The meat then is distributed to relatives and friends of the crew and stored in ice cellars for winter consumption. When the whale hunt is unsuccessful, the men seek smaller game such as seal, duck, and ptarmigan.

In June and July, when the sea ice breaks up, the attention of the hunters shifts to walrus and seal which they pursue in powerboats and skin-covered umiaks. These animals are butchered on the ice and the meat and ivory are carried to the village. Walrus herds of as many as a hundred head drift north with the ice pans along the same route taken by the whale. During these summer months seal, duck, caribou, and fish provide supplemental sources of food.

Immediatly after freeze-up in the fall, the villagers prepare for the period of winter darkness. Where available, local veins of coal are mined and sacked, and driftwood is collected for winter fuel. Houses are repaired and ice is obtained and stored in underground cellars for later use as cooking and drinking water.

Winter introduces the trapping season which extends to the middle of March. In most years, trapping is a minor activity because of the low price of furs, except that of polar bear, which brings as much as $12 a foot. During this period fish are sought in river inlets and seal hunted at their breathing holes. In the times of maximum darkness and severe storms, stored meat and canned goods are the prime sources of food.

The words of an old Barrow Eskimo describe this most difficult season.

> These are the baddest months, maybe for the Eskimo. That is when the animals are the hardest to find. These are the coldest days too. We hunt mostly along the coast, hunt seal. We also hunt polar bear once in awhile. We hunt seal when there are leads in the ice and at their breathing holes. One way is to sit and wait at a hole. It is very hard to do this for long periods. Once I had to wait for four hours.
>
> One of the first times I went out hunting, I saw an *ugrook* put his head up to the hole in the ice to breathe. And I very much wanted to kill an *ugrook,* so I wait and I wait and I wait for him to come up again. The seals were coming up but no *ugrook.* The seals would poke their noses in the hole and I let them breathe. Finally, someone shouted that the ice was breaking at this spot and trying to float me out to sea. So I got up and started to run. I finally reach the shore ice but I never got the *ugrook.* When I got home, I talked with my old dad and told him I saw an *ugrook* at the seal hole, and then that I saw seals there and did not shoot them. I let them breathe. Gee, but my father scolded me. He said, "You went out there to hunt. That's no way to hunt. You are to kill all kinds of animals when they get close to you. After that mistake you won't find any seals in the holes."

With the return of the sun in the spring the north Alaskan Eskimo begin again their seasonal cycle.

Changes in Hunting Patterns

Whale hunting, in addition to providing an important food source, gives strong support to the Eskimo's image of himself as a courageous and daring person—and with good reason. Hunting this largest of mammals is a semifrozen sea is an impressive activity with today's efficient technology, and before the innovation of whale bombs and darting guns, it was even more dramatic.

Aboriginally, the harpoon and lance were the usual weapons. Attached to the harpoon were two or three inflated sealskin pokes, each with a buoyancy of 200 to 300 pounds (Stefansson 1944:102), and a rawhide line connected the floats to the harpoon head. In the spring, boat crews camped on the ice and when a whale was sighted they launched the umiak and approached the animal in such a way that the bow of the boat could be placed on its back, or at least close enough for the harpooner to sink his spear into the thick skin. As other crew members cast floats over the side, the harpooner tried to sink additional spears. The floats had the function both of indicating where the whale was struck and slowing it in its attempts to sound or swim away.

When the whale had become tired, the crew could safely approach and the lancer began his work. The traditional lance was ten to twelve feet in length, tipped with a razor-sharp flint blade. To prevent the whale from sounding, the lancer severed the tendons controlling the whale's flukes, and then probed deeply into its vital organs or pierced a major blood vessel. As the wounded animal went into its death flurry the crew retreated to a safe distance. The dead whale then was hauled onto the sea ice and butchered.

With the arrival of commercial whalers on the north Alaskan coast, the darting gun replaced the harpoon. Its particular advantage was that it carried a small explosive charge which, if well placed, could kill outright, or at least do enough damage to make unnecessary the long and dangerous chase. The shoulder gun, also introduced at this time, soon replaced the lance since it too was more efficient in ensuring a quick kill. By the end of the nineteenth century the traditional weapons had been completely replaced by the darting and shoulder guns.

During the height of the commercial whaling activity the cost of these weapons and ammunition was of little concern since the baleen from a single whale might bring as much as $10,000. After the collapse of the baleen market in the early 1900s the Eskimo still relied on the whale for subsistence and prestige needs, but the cost of ammunition and other supplies effectively limited the number of boat crews hunting each spring. Since the Eskimo either could or would not return to the aboriginal techniques, the number of boats today is governed by a potential crew's ability to raise the $300 to $400 necessary to outfit a boat.

Although there are fewer crews now than in the past, whale hunting is still an important economic activity. Each village along the northwest Alaskan coast has at least two or three crews participating each spring and fall. A crew is made up of the captain or "boat steerer," a "shoulder-gun man," a harpooner or "striker," and three or more paddlers. It usually is composed of extended family members, although this pattern is more flexible today than in the past.

During the hunt, crews maintain fairly close contact, and after a whale has been sighted and killed, other crews assist in towing it to the edge of the ice where members of the village come to help strip the blubber, or flense it. The meat is divided equally, with one portion going to the successful crew, another to the assisting crews, and the third to the village "helpers."

Traditionally there was a rigid set of magical practices and taboos associated with whale hunting. Members of the crew carried amulets, they abstained from cooking in the ice camp, and the shaman performed drumming rites. Today these practices have been replaced by Christian prayers after the whale has been sighted and again after it has been harpooned. Prayers also are offered in church at the beginning of the hunting season, and the success of the hunt may be attributed to these prayers.

Other customs associated with whaling still obtain today. A preliminary feast often is held at the home of the *umialik,* boat captain, for the crew and their families. After the feast there is a procession of the crew members to the edge of the ice. As they set out from the *umialik's* house, they scatter candy to all the children of the village who gather around. The *umialik* continues to be responsible for supplying all the needs of his crew during the whaling season; he must feed them, supply them with cigarettes, and provide ammunition.

Although becoming a whaling *umialik* is still a traditional avenue to gaining prestige, it is barred to those men who do not have a substantial cash income. As well as skill and a willingness to work hard, a modern whaling captain must have the economic capital to purchase all necessary equipment and supplies.

Following the spring whale hunting the Eskimo turn their attention to hunting walrus and seal. During June and July these sea mammals drift north with the ice and can often be found directly in front of the coastal villages from Point Hope to Barrow. Walrus herds numbering between 50 and 100 animals are hunted by boat crews in much the same way as is the whale. Walrus rarely are found at Kaktovik due to the village's eastern location away from the regular migration path. Groups or individuals may hunt the smaller seals. When off-shore wind blows the ice close to the coast, Eskimo even may hunt seal from the shore line.

Seal hunting, although it carries less prestige and provides less meat than the whale or walrus, is the basic staple of the Eskimo subsistence economy. Fluctuations in whale and walrus populations along the north Alaskan coast have always contributed to the subsistence stresses of the Eskimo. Seal, on the other hand, provide essentially the same products as the whale, and are accessible throughout much of the year.

This dependence upon the seal is reflected in the highly developed aboriginal techniques of hunting it. These techniques varied according to the seasonal habits of the seal and the ice conditions. During the winter when the sea is completely frozen over, the seal maintains a series of breathing holes through the ice covering an area of several acres. The Eskimo stationed himself near one of these holes and waited with great patience until the seal surfaced. His harpoon was devised specially so that the head could be detached from the shaft. On sighting a seal he thrust the harpoon down through the narrow opening at the surface of the ice and into the neck or head of the seal. As the seal pulled away, the shaft worked loose from the ivory head. Laying aside the shaft, the Eskimo took hold of the line attached to the harpoon head and pulled the seal to the surface of the ice where it was then killed.

During the late spring and summer months when the seal lay on the surface of the ice, surface stalking was most common. Then the Eskimo ranged over a wide territory and often obtained large numbers of seal in a shorter time. The major problem in this type of hunting was that of the approach. A throwing rather than a thrusting harpoon was used but its effective range was seldom more than twenty-five feet, which called for great skill in stalking. The hunter could approach to within 300 yards of the seal without taking special precautions. He might wear light clothing to camouflage himself against the ice and cloud background, or he might wear dark clothing and try to imitate another seal by moving closer at a much slower pace. By mimicking the seal's movements and timing his advance to accord with the seal's short "naps," a hunter could approach to within a few feet of the seal (Stefansson 1944:252–254).

Because of the time-consuming nature of these aboriginal techniques, the harpoon was replaced by the rifle when it became available. Not only does it kill more quickly, but the seal does not seem to be apprehensive of the crack of a rifle shot. Thus the hunter can take several seal from the same location. One drawback of the rifle is that it does not allow the seal to be easily retrieved. This becomes a particularly difficult problem in late spring and summer when the animals have lost their thick layer of fat and tend to sink when shot. Very often the Eskimo shoots to wound rather than to kill so that he can retrieve the seal before it sinks, and then dispatches it with a quick shot to the head.

The Eskimo's recognition of the efficiency of the harpoon is demonstrated in the techniques used to hunt the large bearded seal. They try to wound it, then get close enough to thrust a harpoon into its body. After retrieving and killing it, they tie the seal to the boat and haul it to shore.

Caribou is the most significant land mammal regularly hunted. Traditionally it provided a variety of food, sinew for sewing, antlers for implements, and skins for clothing, tents, and bedding. Meat and skin were the most important of these items, with skin serving for clothing even up to the present day.

Caribou are sought in the summer, very often near the coast where they are easily accessible to the Eskimo. Aboriginally, caribou herds were driven into rivers, lakes, or corrals where the hunters could most easily ambush and kill them. Less frequently, lone caribou were stalked individually on the open tundra. At this time, the major weapon was the bow and arrow which had an effective range of thirty to fifty yards. Spears and knives were used at an ambush or other close-range kill. It was not until the beginning of the twentieth century when the rifle became a common weapon, that the bow and arrow disappeared.

Caribou frequently are hunted in the fall as well. Often a group of hunters from related families travel inland for several days searching for small herds migrating back toward the interior mountains. After a successful hunt, the Eskimo return to their village to distribute the meat equally among the families of those who made the trip.

Eaten throughout the year, caribou meat constitutes a major source of the Eskimo diet. A full-time hunter with a family of five kills an average of twenty-four caribou each year. The average annual kill at Wainwright is 800 caribou (Milan 1958:28).

Fish also play an important part in providing a stable diet for the Eskimo. Traditionally, fishing was practically a year-round activity. In winter, fish were caught through a hole in the sea ice with a line and lures made of ivory or walrus teeth. A few Eskimo still fish in winter, although the lure may be a small can opener key or similar innovation.

Today, fishing is most important in the late summer and early fall. At this time, Eskimo families often leave the village for their own fish camps along the coast, setting up nets in a good location such as the mouth of a stream or river. In a good season, as many as fifty to seventy-five whitefish or other species may be brought in each day. Any fish not eaten at the time are stored dried or frozen in ice cellars for future use.

In general the yearly cycle of Eskimo subsistence activities has been maintained right up to the present. The changes that have occurred are primarily those relating to techniques used. In many respects the north Alaskan Eskimo have become more dependent on the outside world, not so much for subsistence as for the means to obtain it (see Sonnenfeld 1960). It has been the means rather than the ends that have varied greatly since the early 1900s.

Today, however, this economic picture is changing. Although most north Alaskan Eskimo regularly engage in hunting and fishing, a steadily increasing number are finding fairly permanent salaried jobs in government, military, and other agencies located in the far north. To the extent that most village residents continue to rely on hunting for much of their livelihood, the cooperative effort necessary for success in this activity serves as a major force for community integration. Where the desire and opportunity for salaried income becomes predominant, this traditional integrative influence is reduced proportionally.

Modern Economic Life

Although hunting is still a major economic activity, a stable cash income is increasingly desired. Accessibility of cash is, of course, not new to the north Alaskan Eskimo. Since the early 1900s these people have been handling quite large amounts of money, particularly at the height of the commercial whaling industry and during the peak of the fox fur market.

Nevertheless, the dependence on cash for food, clothing, and other material items became much more pronounced with the advent of World

War II. Furthermore, the way in which they acquired money underwent a dramatic change. Whereas previously they obtained cash from the sale of baleen, fur pelts, or handicrafts, they now usually derive income from short-term wages, salaries, or welfare payments.

The first significant postwar surge in Eskimo employment occurred at Point Barrow in 1946. Two years previously, the United States Navy undertook to explore the possibility of obtaining petroleum in the north Alaskan region. A naval base was established and in 1946 thirty-five Eskimo were hired as laborers. Later, the number increased to eighty. Between 1946 and 1952 from seventy-five to eighty Eskimo were employed regularly at the naval base. Although seasonal layoffs were common, these early economic opportunities had considerable influence on the entire north Alaskan coast. As Eskimo from Wainwright, Point Lay, Kaktovik, and elsewhere moved to Barrow to take advantage of the new jobs, working a sixty-three hour week with time and a half for overtime at regular skilled and semiskilled wages, the economic impact on the cultural life of this village was immense. Motion picture theaters, coffee shops, pool halls, and new stores selling luxury items gave Barrow an entirely new urban character.

Even more dramatic economic and cultural changes followed the initial construction of the DEW Line radar installations across Alaska and the rest of the North American arctic. So many jobs were available that Eskimo from as far away as Aklavik in Canada took up residence near the construction sites. Overtime salaries enabled some Eskimo families to earn as much as $8000 to $10,000 a year, and these incomes continued until the completion of construction in 1957. At some of the larger sites, many jobs are still available and may continue indefinitely since extensive maintenance is required.

Probably the most important economic change that has taken place in those villages having access to steady wage employment has been the shift from hunting and fishing to that of full-time wage work. With this shift, the daily search for food has become both impossible and unnecessary. Furthermore, the traditional mobility so characteristic of the Eskimo living in a somewhat sparse hunting area has been curtailed. Eskimo working for the government on a full-time basis can no longer leave their villages for an inland hunting trip in the spring or fall, or move their families to more attractive fishing gounds in the late summer.

In villages like Kaktovik, where the majority of men work at the nearby DEW Line site, hunting has become a part-time activity generally limited to spring and summer, when game is plentiful and most easily obtained. Nevertheless, seldom is enough food stored away to support a family through the winter months. In this village, all the residents now depend on mail-order houses and other stores to provide them with the major part of their winter food supply; this, in turn, has brought about a great increase in the variety of foods consumed. The still-popular meat and fish diet now is supplemented with a wide variety of fruits, meats, and occasionally, canned vegetables.

In those villages most affected by the full-time wage economy, the decrease of hunting has brought about a corresponding decrease in many activities associated with this pattern. Fewer caribou and sea mammals mean fewer skin boats, native clothing items, tools, and traditional weapons. Young women no longer are trained in the art of skin sewing, nor are the young men able to construct a kayak frame. While caribou parkas and mukluks are standard dress in winter, they are worn over Western clothing. In summer, clothing includes wool suits and cotton dresses for the women and military surplus pants, jackets, and boots for the men.

House styles also have undergone major changes. The traditional driftwood, log, and sod structure has been replaced by the larger two- or three-room home constructed of scrap lumber taken from machinery-packing crates and other available refuse. Government scrap piles are a continual source of amazement to the Eskimo who find a vast assortment of usable items ranging from discarded strips of insulation, to nails, bolts, and wire.

Villages without local access to a cash income have made other adjustments. Point Hope, for example, has a successful mixed economy. Although hunting still fills most subsistence needs, many young people seek summer employment in Fairbanks, Anchorage, or at one of the DEW Line sites. This type of employment has greatly increased the purchasing power of the villagers.

A similar pattern emerges at Wainwright. In 1955, the estimated total income for Wainwright villagers (population 227) was $65,600 (Milan 1958:41). By 1962 this figure had risen to approximately $93,950. Sources and variations in income over this seven-year period are reflected in the table below.

Wainwright: Changing Income Levels, 1955–1962

	1955	1962
Government subsidies	$12,000	$26,037
Salaries and wages	51,600	48,963
Leases, permits, royalties		720
Annuities, interest, dividends		1988
Private businesses		12,130
Native crafts	1000	889
Raw hides sold	1000	323
Native food products sold (fish)		3000
	$65,600	$93,950

These comparative figures clearly demonstrate the increase in government subsidies, the growth of such private businesses as pool halls, movies, stores, and coffee shops, the drop in relative importance of trapping, and the rise in sale of native food products. Salaried income derives primarily from employment in weather observation, the DEW Line, airline agencies, and the local post office.

Although the north Alaskan Eskimo have undergone periods of relative affluence in the past, these recent economic changes have had a far more permanent impact on traditional life patterns. Today, many Eskimo may eat sea mammal and caribou meat along with imported foods, but their tastes are changing. Although the umiak still is used, the number of Eskimo who can construct such a boat are becoming fewer each year. Although hunting and skin sewing are still major sources of prestige for the Eskimo man and woman, respectively, relatively few young people are being adequately trained to perpetuate these skills. The technological changes that have occurred over the past twenty years have resolved some of the basic economic insecurities of the Eskimo. At the same time, they have changed the whole structure of community social life. The character of this change is explored in the next chapter.

4

Village Life

The Modern Setting

MODERN ESKIMO VILLAGES bear little physical resemblence to those of precontact times. The small driftwood frame and sod houses that once symbolized man's habitation of the north Alaskan coast now have been replaced by an assortment of Western-style homes ranging from one-room huts, with a single plastic window or skylight, to well-designed multiroom dwellings. Poorer homes are much like those found in poverty-striken communities far to the south. Constructed of lumber from packing crates, tar paper, and other products of government and military scrap piles, they quickly blunt the romantic idealization of the Eskimo held by many vacationing tourists now beginning to visit these northern communities. Only the more affluent have sufficient salaried income to be able to purchase sawed lumber, plywood, glass windows, and appropriate insulation, all of which must be shipped or flown in from southern urban centers. Regardless of size, each home has an attached storage shed in which hunting equipment, supplies, boots, and other outdoor ware are kept. Those who can afford it heat their homes with fuel oil purchased from the local trader, native store, or military supply dump. The less well to do use driftwood and coal, although fuel oil discarded by DEW Line personnel occasionally is available. With the assistance of the federal government, Barrow village has been able to obtain natural gas for home heating from deposits discovered in the 1940s.

Most houses are built by their owners with the help of extended kin. Due to the high cost of paint and minimal deterioration of wood in this climate, few houses are painted. Entering a typical home a visitor finds several chairs, a table, an oil or wood-burning stove, and numerous bunk beds. Wood or cardboard insulated walls often are covered with

photographs of friends and relatives, religious pictures, and perhaps a calendar provided by one of the many mail-order supply houses. Today, many homes have access to a generating unit providing power for radios, clocks, and similar electrical equipment.

With the exception of the more urban Barrow village, streets are virtually nonexistent. Houses face each other at all possible angles, seemingly without plan. This picture is deceiving, however, as the author learned shortly after his first visit to the north.

Soon after arriving in the small village of Kaktovik, I began a preliminary study of the extended kinship pattern of the local residents. It was early June and the blanket of ice and snow which had covered the village for the past nine months was disappearing rapidly. Initial inquiries into kinship affiliation indicated that extended families lived in attached or separate houses clustered together in various sections of the village. This information was given visual substantiation several weeks later. As the snow melted, the network of village kin ties was clearly portrayed by the now visible electric wires running along the ground from the generators to the various homes. Extended kin shared electricity from a common generator; families without kin had their own separate units.

By late June or early July, many families move from their homes into summer tents. Some place their tents next to their winter homes while other families move out of the village entirely to their summer hunting and fishing camps several miles away.

The present-day diet is a blend of both traditional and modern foods. All Eskimo with sufficient capital are able to buy a wide variety of Western foods at local cooperative or trader's stores. In addition to basic items such as tea, sugar, flour, and canned milk, most families regularly purchase canned fruits, bread and crackers, candy, tobacco, and other easily available goods.

The bulk of the food derives from traditional sources, however. Meat from the whale, seal, and caribou is stored regularly in ice cellars to be available when needed. Much of the meat is prepared by boiling, although large amounts of raw and dried meat also are consumed. Caribou is the preferred food; seal meat is the least desired and usually is reserved for the dogs.

The Eskimo's summer clothing is obtained largely from the so-called wishing book or mail-order catalogue. Men typically wear the shoepack, wool or corduroy pants or jeans, sweater or Western-style jacket, peaked cap, and fur-trimmed parka. Generally, women wear a long cloth *atigi* sufficiently large to accommodate a child on the back. Under this fur-trimmed cloth parka they may have a fur inner lining or sweater and jeans. Most women also wear a bright-colored head scarf and Western shoes or boots. In winter, traditional clothing appears and both men and women wear caribou and sealskin parkas. Sealskin pants or winter-insulated Western clothing are used for hunting trips or other outdoor activities. In addition, most Eskimo have one or more smartly styled suits or dresses which they wear in summer or winter to go to church, ceremonials, or other important village-wide activities. Lipstick, make-up, and Western hair styles are becoming increasingly common among adolescents and younger women.

Family routine varies considerably with the season. Families with school-age youngsters often rise by seven-thirty or eight o'clock in the morning so that the children may reach classes on time. In most homes, the three meals-a-day plan has been adopted, at least during the school year. If the father has a salaried job nearby, he may join his children for the noon meal. In the evening, dinner is served when the father returns from hunting or from his work.

In June, at the close of school, the household routine becomes far more irregular, and strict schedules seldom are kept. Sleeping habits also vary, particularly among adolescents who may stay up all night and sleep all day. Meals are makeshift and rarely does the entire family eat at one time. If children are out playing they may not even be called, the assumption being that they will come in when they get hungry.

The typical meal consists of boiled, raw, or frozen meat, crackers and bread, tea, and perhaps a side dish of fruit. Boiled meat often is prepared with cooked rice and seal oil.

When the food is on the table, the men and boys help themselves first, followed by the girls and finally the mother. Because of the scarcity of chairs, the family members may stand, sit on the edge of the bunk bed, or find some other temporary seating arrangement.

Evenings usually are taken up with chores around the home, church service, visits to other homes, or perhaps to a movie in the local church, armory, or theater. Members of recently introduced fundamentalistic church groups may attend evening services as many as four or five nights a week.

On Sundays, work is considered inappropriate. Families attend church and Sunday school, visit, play cards, or participate in other leisure-time activities. Indeed, there are so many community-wide events taking place each week that some Eskimo complain their social life is overorganized, a view not unlike that expressed by southern suburbanites.

Marriage, Family, and Kin

Aboriginally, the bilaterally extended family was the basic unit of north Alaskan Eskimo social structure. The recognition of kin through at least three generations on both the mother's and father's side of the family, combined with the extensive geographical mobility of the people of this region, provided an interwoven pattern of kinship linking together most villages. By means of a system of economic partnership, quasi-kinship groups were also formed, effectively extending cooperative ties to nonkin as well. Under this arrangement, all Eskimo who called each other by real or fictive kinship terms assumed a relation of sharing and cooperation (the extent of obligation depending on degree of distance from ego), and were seen by outsiders as being responsible for the actions of the entire kin group. Feuds occasionally arose between these groups and when the conflict resulted in murder, retaliation required the joint action of the appropriate kin members.

Today, many traditional functions of the extended family and of economic partnerships have declined in importance. Effective government control over interfamily feuding has removed the need for mutual protection of kin. Economic interdependence has lessened as opportunities for individual wage labor become more frequent. The desire for economic gain draws many Eskimo away from their traditional communities to more urban centers, and few of these migrants feel a strong obligation to give even a small portion of their income to relatives outside the immediate family. Economic affluence within the community and extensive migration are the two most important factors contributing to the decline of the extended family. At present, cooperative kin ties are seen most commonly in the secondary economic activities of baby-sitting, butchering meat, setting and checking fish nets, loading and unloading boats, preparing ice cellars, painting houses, and sharing common household items. In each of these instances cooperation is expected, and if a request goes unheeded, the individual may become an object of gossip.

Traditionally, the choice of a marriage partner appears to have varied considerably from one village to another. In some communities such as Point Hope, Kaktovik, and Wainwright, parallel or cross-cousin marriage was preferred; while at Barrow, marriage between first cousins was much less common (Spencer 1959). Regardless of the traditional pattern, most young people today are free to choose their own partners with few restrictions or parental strictures. Occasionally, negative feelings may be expressed regarding the formation of cousin marriages, because the Eskimo have wondered about the possible deleterious effects of these marriages on the children. First-cousin marriage is not considered immoral, though, and in small villages with a limited number of eligible spouses, it is fairly common.

Wife exchange, at one time a characteristic feature of Eskimo life, is no longer practiced. Traditionally, two men could agree to exchange their wives, particularly if they were good friends and had known each other for a long time. Partners in spouse exchange called each other *aiparik*, "the second," and their children used a reciprocal term *qatang* for each other. Significantly, those individuals who were *qatang* had definite obligations toward one another similar to those between brothers and sisters.

Today, the youngest Eskimo using these terms are at least forty years of age (Milan 1958:50).

Although formalized wife exchange has disappeared, modern sexual mores are, by Western standards, still relatively free. As viewed by a local missionary, Eskimo attitudes are "halfway between the old and new." Although the more conservative elders and other leaders of the local churches encourage their young people to marry before they become sexually involved, this advice often is bypassed and many young couples do not marry until they have children. This pattern is due largely to two factors—first, economic responsibilities of marriage make demands which many young Eskimo men find difficult to meet; and second, some young men are reluctant to marry when they already have a relatively large degree of sexual liberty outside the marriage bond.

When a couple decides to marry, they usually make arrangements with the local missionary to hold the ceremony in the village church. Even in remote inland villages most couples are now married by a minister or priest. The old custom, whereby a young man and woman simply established their own household without regard to the marriage ceremony, is extremely rare today. Even older couples whose common-law arrangement is accepted by missionaries, government personnel, and other whites in the community, are encouraged to go through a legal ceremony to ensure the inheritance rights of their children.

Changes in courtship and marriage patterns now taking place are related primarily to opportunities for wage employment and the greater mobility of young people. In the modern world prestige and eligibility as a suitor are measured more by the young man's wage-earning abilities than by his skill as a hunter. For this reason, many young men leave their own communities for jobs at Barrow, Fairbanks, or other villages and towns offering salaried employment. This mobility seriously disturbs the sex ratio of the smaller villages.

Following the marriage ceremony, most young couples set up initial residence with the family of the bride or groom. This arrangement eases the economic responsibilities of the new couple and also helps them learn the techniques and skills needed to support and maintain their family.

The division of labor among adults is much like that described for teen-agers. Such traditional activities as meat butchering and skin sewing are undertaken by older women rather than girls, and most of the ordinary cloth sewing also is done by older women. However, female members of every household cooperate in normal day-to-day activities such as tending babies, washing dishes and clothes, cleaning, cooking, getting water, chopping wood, and burning trash.

In some of these tasks, such as obtaining wood and water, the male members of the household also help. Men may assist in setting up tents and drying racks, making windbreaks for butchering meat, filling fuel tanks, and starting recalcitrant washing machines. Women tend to play an auxiliary role in these jobs as long as men are available to do the major part of the work. If the men are not available, the women undertake the task themselves. In theory, there are domains which are predominantly male such as sea-mammal and caribou hunting, running boats, and doing the heaviest household chores; female domains include doing indoor house-work, caring for children, butchering meat, and sewing skins. Nevertheless, members of each sex know the other's skills and can perform these roles when necessary.

Eskimo attitudes toward the division of labor are portrayed clearly in the following statement of a fifty-year-old Barrow male.

> The women are supposed to take care of the house. A man does the hunting, a woman takes care of the kids and the food. She should know how much they got left, how much food there is for the kids. They always check the food. A man is always asking his wife "how much have you got left?" And the woman says, "we have so much, to last us so many days or weeks." The woman always takes care of the food, and sews or patches clothes for the husband and the kids. She also scrapes all the caribou skin, seal, or whatever the skin is. But the man must help too once in a while. When we are a little short of food, the man spends most of his time hunting. The man never cooks or feeds the children be-cause he hunts every day. Although the women are supposed to take care of the house and the kids, they sometimes help the men too. Women go up river to hunt the ptarmigan while the men are hunting caribou. My wife was always known as a good shooter. She killed lots of ptarmigan and even went seal hunting with me sometimes. Once in a while when the women do not have a lot of children to take care of, they may even go out by themselves and hunt the caribou in the summer time. In win-ter, when the children are inside, women don't do much hunting.

Interpersonal relations between husband and wife in the home con-trast sharply with those of Anglo-American society. Spouses seldom display any feelings of emotion in the other's presence and conversation tends to center around material problems of the household. Even when the husband prepares to leave on an extended hunting trip, his wife expresses very little emotion about his departure. Nor does she necessarily welcome him home, other than to assist in unloading the sled and carrying in the meat. She may, however, find other nonverbal ways of communicating her feelings of pleasure on his return.

Although economic considerations play a major role in consolidating the marriage relationship, the bond between husband and wife is not entirely limited to this sphere. In most instances, couples enjoy one another's companionship, and hold each other in mutual affection and respect. They often assist or instruct one another in various activities. Young men teach their wives how to shoot or flense a caribou. A wife offers pointers to her husband on how to improve the butchering of a seal or *ugrook*. This cooperative pattern is found in all Eskimo villages irrespective of the degree of family acculturation.

Outside the economic sphere, separation of the sexes in village social life is more pronounced. Couples seldom go visiting together, although in the course of an evening social round, both husband and wife may find themselves in the same house. Nor do they entertain friends jointly. Gatherings which are predominantly female are largely ignored by any men present except for an occasional comment or joke. Often, if several women enter a home, the men will get up and leave. In situations which are predominantly male, the women assume a passive role and remain in the background. A woman whose husband is entertaining friends may serve tea, listen to the conversation, laugh at appropriate occasions, and perhaps ask a question, but she rarely participates actively in the conversation. When the group is more or less evenly mixed, as when people are invited to hear a recorded tape-letter from a friend or relative, the companionable exchange is primarily among members of the same sex.

Informal visiting is an important feature of daily family life. A friend may drop in on a neighbor, simply stand around for a few minutes, and then leave with little or no announcement of his departure or expression of farewell. A visitor may enter a house and, after giving an initial greeting, ignore its occupants; he or she may sit and read a mail-order catalogue or a religious tract, or simply watch the activities of the household. Though efforts to entertain the guest are minimal he usually is asked to have a cup of tea or coffee and crackers, the standard mid-morning or afternoon snack.

If getting away from one's home is an important form of relaxation among the Eskimo, a trip away from the village is even more enjoyable. The common distinction made between "recreation" and "work" is nowhere as pronounced among the Eskimo. Trips away from the village may have as their prime purpose hunting, checking the fish net, collecting snow from ice flows for drinking water, and doing other useful activities, but camping trips and extended boat rides are likely to be perceived as a "vacation" or "rest." Therefore they are an attractive break in the day-to-day round of household activities.

Other Social Groups

The core of traditional Eskimo social life centered around the individual's nuclear and extended family, a relationship continually reinforced by patterns of mutual aid and reciprocal obligation. Beyond this extended circle of kin, there existed other more voluntary associations, such as trading and joking partnerships, hunting groups, and the *karigi*, or men's ceremonial dance and club houses. It was through participation in these latter institutions that the Eskimo developed a sense of identity with a particular settlement or village.

In both the inland caribou- and coastal-whale-hunting groups, by far the most dominant figure was the *umialik*, or hunting group leader. Men of great wealth and high social position, these individuals were powerful community leaders, a trait shared only with the religious shamans. Indeed, many *umialik* were shamans as well. Though not accorded any formally defined authority, they won the right to rule through their personal attributes of modesty, honesty, and hunting skill, reinforced by sufficient wealth to support a boat crew or hunting group. These qualities were requisite to keeping such a group intact, since membership was voluntary and could be altered at any time.

Modern boat crews differ little from those of earlier times, and the *umialik* still supplies his crew with up-to-date whale hunting equipment, food, and other needed materials. For his leadership and his organizational and financial investments he always receives the largest share of the whale meat, which he then either divides among his family and extended kin, trades, or sells.

The *karigi,* on the other hand, have all but disappeared. Prior to the arrival of Christian missionaries, every north Alaskan Eskimo village had one or more of these ceremonial dance houses. Membership was determined by one's association with a particular hunting crew. Children joined the house of their father, and on marriage a woman transferred to that of her spouse. During the spring and fall, dances, games, and feasts sponsored by the *umialiks* and their crews were held regularly in the *karigi.* As well as serving as the center for ceremonials associated with hunting, the *karigi* were meeting places for men. With the opening of the ceremonial season in the fall, men spent most of the day there in work and recreation. The wives brought food to them and sometimes remained to participate in games or dances. Occasionally men and their older sons slept in the *karigi* as well.

Recreational activities reached their peak in midwinter. Games of physical strength, gambling, storytelling, and string-figures were common. Friendly competition between different *karigi* groups was encouraged, and implemented by wrestling matches and contests in weight lifting, jumping, chinning a bar, miniature bow and arrow shoots, and kickball.

Another popular wintertime activity of the *karigi* was dancing, which took several forms. Some dances, limited to men, portrayed a particular event, such as the search for polar bear or a joke played on a friend. Women's dances were usually more static, consisting of rhythmical movements of hands and body performed in a given location. Sometimes couples danced in unison or as part of a larger group. Today mimicry in a dance is common, and it often reflects the seemingly foolish actions of local whites.

Accompaniment was provided by several drummers, beating tambourine-type drums and humming. The blend of the beat and the rhythmical rise and fall of voices, punctuated with shouts of *auu yah iah,* quickly drew *karigi* members to the dance floor.

One of the most important annual festivals held at the *karigi* was the Messenger Feast. Usually held in December, it was a ceremony with both social and economic significance. In early winter, an *umialik* of a given community sent messengers to a nearby village to invite the residents to participate in an economic exchange. Because of the expense, no one community could afford to give such a feast each year. The choice of the invited village usually was based on the number of trading and joking partners involved and the length of time lapsed since the previous invitation. Elaborate gift exchange between village residents added further to the development of intercommunity solidarity, as did the opportunity for distant kin to re-establish social and economic ties while participating in the activities of the feast.

Today, the *karigi* are no longer significant ceremonial centers. None remain at Barrow or Wainwright. There are two at Point Hope, but they are meaningful only in so far as they affect the patterning of the Christmas and spring whaling feasts (VanStone 1962:102). Nor is the Messenger Feast of current ceremonial importance, with only a vestige of the festival being held between Christmas and New Year's Day.

The one traditionally important annual ceremony still actively followed today is the *nalukatak,* or spring whale festival. Arrangements for this celebration, which takes place at the end of the whaling season, are made by the successful *umialiks* and their families. If no whales have been caught, there is no ceremony. Formerly, the festival took place in a *karigi* as was an attempt to propitiate the spirits of the deceased whales and ensure through magical means the success of future hunting seasons. A modern adaptation of this religious belief is seen on those occasions when Christian prayers of thanksgiving are recited during the ceremony.

On the day chosen for the event, all boat crews who have killed one or more whales during the season haul their umiaks out of the sea and drag them to the ceremonial site. The boats then are turned on their sides to serve as windbreaks and temporary shelter for the participants, and braced with paddles or forked sticks. Masts are erected at the bow and from the top are flown the small bright-colored flags of each successful *umialik*. Before Christian teachings changed the practice, the captain placed his hunting charms and amulets on these masts. When the site has been arranged completely and a prayer given, the families of the *umialik* cut off the flukes and other choice sections of the whale, and distribute them along with tea, biscuits, and other food, to all invited guests.

After a period of general relaxation, informal conversation, and further serving of meat and tea, the *nalukatak* skin, or "skin for tossing," is brought out. Of all the Eskimo cermonial customs, the *nalukatak* or "blanket toss" is perhaps most well known to whites; and it is an exciting affair to watch.

When they bring out the "skin," thirty or more Eskimo take their places in a circle, grasping firmly with both hands the rope handgrips or rolled edge. The object of the game is to toss a person into the air as high as possible which is sometimes more than twenty feet. This individual must then keep his balance and return upright to the blanket. Usually the first to be tossed are the successful *umialiks*. Traditionally, they were expected, while high in the air, to throw out gifts of baleen, tobacco, and other items to the crowd, and even today candy is sometimes used as a substitute. Once an individual loses his footing, another takes his place, until all have had a chance to participate.

In the late afternoon or evening, a dance is scheduled. When a permanent dance floor or temporary board platform has been made ready, five or ten male drummers, supported by a chorus of men and women, announce the beginning of the dance. The first dance, called the *umialikit*, is obligatory for the *umialik*, his wife, and crew. All other crews then dance in turn, followed by other men and women in the village. The affair often lasts well into the night.

Several United States national holidays, including Thanksgiving, Christmas, New Year's Day, and the Fourth of July, are celebrated by the Eskimo. On the Fourth of July, for example, there are foot races for the children, kayak and other boat races for the men, and a concluding fireworks display. In villages situated near military or other government installations, local whites are invited to participate in such Western games as volleyball, baseball, and tug of war. Prizes consist of candy, ice cream, and canned foods.

Thanksgiving is celebrated by a feast in the local village church, followed by group singing, drumming, and dancing. Between Christmas and the New Year, there is a continuous round of games, feasts, church services, drum dances, and dog races. In recent years, several of the newly established churches, among them the Assembly of God, have prohibited all forms of dancing for their members, which has resulted in the separation of some of the more social festivities along religious lines.

In addition to the four major ceremonials in the annual cycle (*nalukatak*, the Fourth of July, Thanksgiving, and Christmas), there is another regularly scheduled event that is important to the life of most coastal villages: the arrival of the supply ship *North Star* in late August or early September. Its significance stems from the fact that it brings together members of the entire community in a concentrated group effort. Men, women, and children all work together beside white longshoremen, unloading yearly supplies for the native stores and schools, and all join in communal meals prepared and eaten in the local store. Actually this occasion, lasting thirty-six to forty-eight hours, involves a greater total community effort than any other single event.

At the more informal recreational level, common social activities include attending local movies, playing pool and cards, visiting kin and friends, organizing picnics, and walking on the beach. At Barrow and other large villages, there are movies shown three or more nights a week. Pool halls are crowded each evening except Sunday, when they do not open until midnight. The various church groups represented in the village usually organize picnics, which teen-agers are likely to attend regardless of religious affiliation. In the summer, volleyball, baseball, and other outdoor games attract players and spectators.

On a typical summer evening, young children range through the village, playing in small groups or watching elders until ten or eleven o'clock, when their older sisters or parents put them to bed. Adults follow soon after they finish with whatever butchering, fish-net repairing, or other chores they have been doing. When the weather is good, small groups of women may stand on the cliff edge or high rise of land, chatting for a while, and watching for the return of their husbands who may be out fishing or hunting. But adults seldom stay up past midnight. After twelve o'clock, the out of doors belongs to the teen-ager. Except in those communities with effective curfews imposed by a village council, the young people regularly stay up until three o'clock or later, walking along the beach, drinking coke or coffee with friends, dancing, playing cards, singing, or visiting each others homes.

Religious diversification, steadily increasing in recent years, has made its impact on village social life. The older Presbyterian or Episcopal and newer evangelical church groups, such as the Assembly of God, differ markedly with regard to the kinds of recreation and social activities they consider moral. Converts to the new denominations, of which there is usually only one in each village, spend far more time in specific church activities than do members of the established congregations. At Wainwright and Kaktovik, for example, services in the Assembly of God Church are often held three hours a night, six nights a week. Although they meet less frequently, Presbyterian members have their own prayer and study groups, sewing circles, and midweek services which do not involve members of other denominations.

Establishing a second church in these villages either creates or more frequently crystallizes splits between different segments of the population in such a way as to reduce the degree of homogeneity. This situation is reflected in the remark of a Wainwright Presbyterian elder who commented: "We used to have good parties until the other church came. We played Eskimo games, danced, played guitars, and sang . . . they have a lo-o-ot of commandments over there—just like the Pharisees, yes?" Converts to the new churches, on the other hand, view many Presbyterians as living a less than moral life. The apparently profound satisfaction with which these recent converts engage in their religious and church affairs attests to their strong sense of what constitutes correct and moral behavior.

Religion and Health

There appears to be little contradiction in the mind of the Eskimo between many of his traditional religious beliefs and those of Christianity. Certainly, most villagers feel themselves to be staunch supporters of the Christian church, though they are aware that *tanniks* do not share all of their aboriginal beliefs, and are therefore cautious about admitting them to outsiders.

Many Eskimo still believe in *inyakuns* (little people who inhabit the region), *makkiligaaroks* (monsters), the ten-legged polar bear, and other supernatural beings. Children speak more openly of these creatures than do adults, but there is little doubt that the youngsters learned of them from their elders. Fear of these beings becomes noticeably stronger in the autumn when darkness increases. A recent *inyakun* "incident" took place at Wainwright when a small girl failed to appear home at bedtime. Many community members spent the night searching for her, sure that she had been carried off in some mysterious manner. Actually, the girl, afraid of being punished for a misdeed, had run away from home and was asleep in a box under another house. The following day, the anthropologist in the community at the time was reproved by the expressions and tones of voice of two relatively acculturated Eskimo, for referring so lightly to the event.

In giving Eskimo names to their children, parents often choose that of a recently deceased person, and they sometimes follow the same pattern in giving English names. Older people may occasionally refer to little children by kin terms appropriate to the individual for whom the child was named, that is, a woman referring to her niece as "mother," but it is difficult to determine whether this is a form of teasing, or whether it reflects the aboriginal belief in name souls.

One of the easiest ways for the anthropologist to gain information on Eskimo religious beliefs is to ask the old people to relate some of the myths and legends that have been passed down from generation to generation. A common myth told to the author by a key informant from Barrow, illustrates the animistic nature of Eskimo religion.

Once there was a poor hunter. He always went out but never got anything. Finally one day he saw a polar bear. As he crawled toward it over the ice, the bear said to him, "Don't shoot me. If you follow me and do what I say, I will make it so you will always be able to get whatever animals you think about." The bear told the man to climb on his back and close his eyes. "Do not open them until I tell you to." Then, the man and the bear went down into the sea a long way. "Do not open your eyes," the bear reminded him. Finally, they came back up and the man saw an igloo along the edge of the pack. They went inside and the man saw another bear with a spear in his haunch. The first bear said, "If you can take that spear out of the bear and make him well, you will become a good hunter." The man broke off the shaft, eased the spear point out of the bear's haunch, and the wound began to heal. Then the first bear took off his bearskin "parka" and became a man. After the wound was healed completely, the bear-man put back on his bearskin "parka," told the poor hunter to climb on his back and close his eyes, and together they went back into the sea. When the bear finally stopped he asked the man to open his eyes. Looking around, the man realized he had been returned to the spot from which he began his journey. He thought he had only been gone a day, but on arriving home, he found that he had been away a month. From then on, the man was always a good hunter.

In this, and in many other myths, spirits of an animistic nature represented the controlling powers. Essentially, the Eskimo perception of the universe was one of internal harmony of the elements in which the various natural and supernatural forces were neutrally disposed toward man. By means of ritual and magic, however, the Eskimo could influence the supernatural forces toward a desired end, be it controlling the weather and food supply, ensuring protection against illness, or curing illness when it struck. The power to influence these events came from the use of charms, amulets, and magical formulas, observance of taboos, and the practice of sorcery.

Although all individuals had access to supernatural power, some were thought to be specially endowed. With proper training, these individuals became practicing *angakoks* or shamans. The Eskimo shaman was a dominant personality and powerful leader in every settlement, as he has been in every society supporting this type of religious practitioner. Due to his great intimacy with the world of the supernatural, he was considered particularly well qualified to cure the sick, control the forces of nature, and predict future events. At the same time, he also was believed to have the power to bring illness, either to avenge some actual or imagined wrong, or to profit materially from its subsequent cure.

The Eskimo of this region traditionally saw illness as resulting from one of two major causes: the loss of one's soul or the intrusion of a foreign object. An individual's soul could wander away during his sleep, be taken away by a malevolent shaman, or leave because he had failed to follow certain restrictions placed on him by a shaman or his culture. Illness caused by intrusion was usually the work of a hostile shaman, but, in either case, an effective cure for a serious illness could only be achieved through the services of a competent nature curer (Spencer 1959:327–330).

Though the shaman had extensive powers, the lay Eskimo was not without his own sources of supernatural influence. By means of various songs, charms, magical incantations, and even names, individuals could ensure the desired end. The acquisition of these instruments of supernatural power came through inheritance or purchase, with charms and songs changing hands most easily and often.

The major difference between the shaman and lay Eskimo was the greater degree of supernatural power assumed to be held by the former. The shaman did have one particular advantage—access to a *tunraq*— or "helping spirit." Similar to the concept of guardian spirit found throughout many North American Indian tribes, the *tunraq* usually was an animal spirit, often a land mammal that could be called upon at any time to assist the shaman. When it was to the shaman's advantage, it was believed that he might also turn himself into the animal represented by the spirit.

The showmanship skills of the shaman were no less dramatic than their apparent supernatural ones. During the months of winter darkness, shamans were most active, frequently demonstrating their powers before others in a *karigi* or patient's home. Called in to cure an illness, the shaman might begin by placing himself in a trance in much the same manner that seances are begun in other cultures. While in this trance, he could speak with a deceased relative of the patient, fly through the air in search of a soul, do battle with the spirit of another shaman, or otherwise demonstrate the extent of his supernatural powers. In the 1880s Charles Brower, the famous white trader living at Barrow observed a Point Hope shaman at work and wrote: "Without waiting for dim lights or any such frills, he proceeded to work himself into a trance on the spot. As I stood by watching his dark, contorted features while he writhed on the floor, it wasn't hard to believe that the instructions issuing forth came straight from the devil in person." (Brower 1942:57)

Although these seances characteristically contained ventriloquism, slight-of-hand, and induced frenzy, there is reason to assume that most Eskimo *angakoks* sincerely believed in their own supernatural powers. A frequently raised question concerns the extent to which these bizarre actions were manifestations of hysterical or neurotic behavior. Certainly, in the role of shaman, the schizoid type of personality could find a culturally approved outlet for his emotions and behavior, not to mention significant material rewards. Throughout Alaska and all of the western arctic, the shaman seldom sought out the role. Rather, an older shaman selected as an apprentice a youth who exhibited behavior that might qualify him for the role. The youth could decline the invitation if he so wished; if he accepted, he was trained in the profession, purchased the appropriate songs, and began his practice. If he was of unstable personality—and this does not apply to all apprentices—the profession at least gave him the opportunity to channel his behavior in an acceptable direction.

The influence of the shaman began to decline following the arrival of white whalers who, without regard for the numerous taboos rigidly enforced by the Eskimo shamans, consistently killed large numbers of whales. The whalers were followed in the mid-1890s by Protestant missionaries, some trained in medicine. Under an arrangement reached by the Federal Council of Churches, north Alaska was divided into several regions; the Barrow-Wainwright, and later the Anaktuvuk Pass, area was assigned to the Presbyterians, and the Point Hope-Point Lay region fell to the Episcopalians. By offering a set of religious beliefs less tinged with anxiety and fear, accompanied by food, clothing, and medical care, the new missionaries quickly were able to replace the shamans as the dominant religious figures (see Spencer 1959:381). Today, shamanism rarely is practiced in northern Alaska. This does not mean, however, that individuals once known to be shamans, or capable of becoming shamans, are ignored. On the contrary, the Eskimo feel quite uneasy about such people.

The reason for this fear is related to the syncretic blending of aboriginal and Christian religious beliefs. The modern Eskimo conceive of the supernatural world as being composed of God, Satan, and numerous vaguely defined devils. The belief in many devils is not only an aboriginal residue, but is actually in perfect conformity with the version of Christianity now presented to these people. Several missionaries in the region preach of the physical existence of devils. Furthermore, the Eskimo believe that shaman's helping powers (*tanraqs*) were real spirits and, by implication, that the shamans actually performed the feats they claim. It follows, therefore, that a shaman who becomes a Christian does not reveal himself as having been an imposter, nor does he necessarily stop being a shaman. Rather, he must exorcise his powers, "send away" the helping spirits, or in some other way, "get rid of them." By equating the *tunraqs* with devils in modern Christian cosmology, it is hardly surprising that the traditional attitude of uneasiness toward shamans still is manifest today. This syncretism further is seen in the present-day belief that some psychotic episodes are attributed to possession by devils. At Wainwright several years ago, an Eskimo minister was called in to pray over an individual who had a "fit" in an attempt to exorcise his devils—a request not unlike that made of a shaman fifty years ago.

The Presbyterian and Episcopal churches in the region have been joined by several new denominations; Assembly of God missionaries have established churches in Barrow and Kaktovik, and Evangelical Friends and other sect missionaries exert some influence in the area of Point Hope. All of these church groups stress of efficacy of prayer—that is, the immediate intervention of God in daily affairs. This intervention usually is asked in the two major areas of hunting and health. All churches preach that God can heal directly, although the evangelical churches preach this doctrine more dramatically. Presbyterians, for example, may use prayer as a supplement to medicine, whereas the Assembly of God members frequently reverse the emphasis. In the Presbyterian Church the minister or the congregation as a whole may be asked to pray for an ill member. In the Assembly of God church, any small group of members regardless of status may be called upon to help "lay on (healing) hands" when someone is sick.

Faith healing is an integral part of evangelical doctrine and examples of success in this endeavor are frequently cited by Eskimo converts. A young boy mangled in the treads of a tractor and given up for dead was prayed over, after which he got up and walked home seemingly without ill effects. A woman who was extremely ill with tuberculosis was sent to the hospital for further examination and rest. After prayers were said for her, the illness immediately disappeared. A man, caught in an avalanche of snow in the mountains, prayed, and was saved from death. Films portraying the faith healing of Oral Roberts and other evangelical ministers are occasionally shown by local missionaries or lay Eskimo preachers, and they dramatically reinforce belief in the immediate efficacy of prayer.

Services differ significantly according to the church in question. The formal service of the Presbyterian and Episcopal churches de-emphasizes individual participation, whereas the evangelical churches encourage personal religious expression. A typical Assembly of God service begins with the singing of revival hymns to the accompaniment of an organ or guitar.

Individual and group prayers and the offering of personal "testimonials" follow. As many as 75 percent of the congregation may stand one at a time to speak in an emotion-laden voice. Each relates the story of his "salvation," enumerating in detail such past sins as drinking, dancing, playing cards, and smoking (women tend to be less specific than men in this regard)—and why he or she will refrain from committing such actions in the future.

Prior to the arrival of the evangelical and sect missionaries, each village had one established church. There is little question that the homogeneity of religious belief arising from this arrangement helped to create a sense of community identity and spirit. Regular services brought together most village residents to share in a common ceremony; the establishment of local church offices provided opportunities for the emergence of new leaders; and a common doctrine set a standard by which individuals could measure their own religious and moral behavior. Resentment against others also found expression in the act of refusing to attend church—effective because such attendance was one of the few activities expected of all village residents. Only subsistence hunters and salaried men assigned work on Sunday could be considered exempt.

As the new denominations and sects gain ground in these communities, religious factionalism becomes more pronounced. Old doctrines are questioned, and new ones debated with the result that the established Presbyterian and Episcopal churches are no longer the unifying force for social cohesion that they were previously. At the same time, the modern Eskimo obtains a more realistic picture of varying forms of Christianity as practiced in the outside world, and having this knowledge, he is better prepared to become a part of that world.

Health practices are also a mixture of old and new, depending partly on the degree of acculturation and the availability of clinic and hospital services. As long ago as the early 1940s the isolated village of Kaktovik received occasional visits from a traveling public health nurse. An older resident, commenting on the problems of tuberculosis at that time, spoke of preventive measures taken: "I never knew much about the sickness, but people took good care of themselves. Each man had his own cup and after every meal he would carefully clean it. All the cups were boiled, each having its own mark and only used by one person."

A study of Kaktovik undertaken in 1958 showed that over 90 percent of the adult villagers had had at least one contact with a physician each year and many had been to the Public Health Service hospital at Barrow for physical examinations, x-rays, or childbirth. Further insight into modern medical beliefs and practices has been gained through contact with resident and visiting public health nurses, DEW Line medical aids, and local school and adult health-education training programs. In communities like Wainwright with limited treatment facilities, reliance on Western medicine is less pronounced. Nevertheless, common drugs and medicines are stored in every school to be dispensed by the teacher or appointed Eskimo "health aids," antibiotics and aspirin being the most widely used remedies.

Some traditional practices continue side by side with the new. Both liniment and rancid seal oil may be used as chest rubs for coughs; actually, liniment may have been adopted because of its similarity to seal oil. Aboriginal remedies now used less often include the application of urine to stanch bleeding and the use of herbal teas for intestinal disorders. Although many women would like to have their babies in a hospital, problems of transportation ensure the continuation of midwifery in the isolated areas. The less acculturated still observe taboos associated with pregnancy, such as not going through a door backwards or not tying strings around the body.

One important reason for the change from traditional beliefs about health to those of Western medicine is that the Eskimo had virtually no intellectual and professional medical system to unlearn. In this area particularly, emphasis was placed on keeping, rather than getting, well. A pragmatic willingness to try new techniques and recognition of the increase in village health problems, which are concomitant with permanent residence in villages and deteriorating sanitary conditions, have lent further support to the acceptance of these new ideas.

Leadership Patterns

A leader usually is defined as the individual who exerts the greatest amount of voluntarily accepted influence on the members of a given group. Prior to extensive white contact, the most significant Eskimo group was the extended family. The eldest male assumed a position of leadership within his kin group, with the amount of his influence determined by his good judgment, industriousness, and generosity. Within the kin group younger men also could assume leadership positions deriving from their skill in hunting, physical strength, stamina, and good judgment. The whale boat *umialik* was clearly a recognized leader, but to the extent that his crew was composed of extended and quasi-kin, the degree of his influence was limited. Probably the most dominant aboriginal leader was the shaman, since his influence consistently extended beyond the kin group to the village at large, and in addition, he had another distinct leadership trait—the ability to generate fear in his followers.

In the late 1800s the white whalers brought many changes to Eskimo technology, economy, health, and population distribution, but the aboriginal patterns of leadership remained comparatively intact. Only on rare instances did traditional kin-group leaders come together to deal with village-wide problems (see Milan 1958:60).

More dramatic social changes began to appear in the early 1900s as missionaries, school teachers, and other whites undertook to Westernize the Eskimo. By 1920, trapping had replaced whaling as the primary source of cash income. This activity, involving long trips away from the village, disrupted kin ties, winter ceremonials, and other cohesive forms of community life. Between 1930 and 1945, the Eskimo were forced by economic necessity to return to their traditional subsistence economy, albeit aided by minor sources of income from trapping or common labor. Cooperative work and social patterns re-emerged and except for the replacement of the shaman by the lay minister, Eskimo leadership retained much of its traditional flavor. At this time the Eskimo were poor in economic wealth and health, but they did have a large measure of autonomy over their own affairs. Western influence generally was limited to the activities of the resident school teachers, missionaries, traders, and, occasionally, health and welfare officers.

Following World War II, new economic and educational opportunities drew many Eskimo to the larger villages and towns, which resulted in the extended family groups becoming less cohesive and their leaders less influential. One of the most serious problems facing all Eskimo communities today is the disruption of traditional kin-group mechanisms of social control, a problem compounded by the steadily declining influence of the older kin-group leaders.

Leadership traits vary with the characteristics of the group and the situation in which the group functions, and it is noteworthy that, except for those traditional activities still carried on in the villages, most of the formal groups have been instigated by whites. These include village councils, church groups, National Guard units, native cooperative store shareholders, unions, sanitary aid teams, Boy and Girl Scout troops, Parent-Teacher Associations, and "mother's clubs." In general these groups operate within a Western organizational framework, drawing up regulations, forming committees, nominating delegates, and assigning tasks. The following are examples:

At Wainwright, the village council organizes the July Fourth celebration. A committee of twelve men and women collect prizes from local householders and supervise the projected games. The Presbyterian women's organization undertakes the preparation and sale of food at the games.

Such church groups as the young people's club, women's sewing circle, and governing committees sponsor village picnics and feasts.

The Presbyterian Church has a committee of Elders, a group of Deacons, and a men's club, each meeting regularly to perform specified functions. Other church groups include a proselytizing committee, the "counters," who note church attendance and post the results on the bulletin board at the back of the church, and "janitors," young people appointed each week to clean. Churches also have informally organized groups that hold Sunday services in the homes of the sick.

The native store organizes the unloading of the supply ship *North Star*, assigning shift work, determining wages, and arranging for the workers' meals.

As contacts with whites increase the requirements of the leadership role become more complex. In addition to being technically proficient at the appropriate task, initiating and directing action, and showing consideration for followers, the Eskimo leader must have an overt awareness of the conflicting patterns and values of white and Eskimo culture and be able to deal effectively with them.

This requires not only a sufficient command of English, but an adequate understanding of those aspects of white society that have a bearing on community life in the north. Fortunately, experience contributing to this understanding has become more widespread in recent years. The Eskimo are becoming better educated, are traveling more to white population centers like Fairbanks and Anchorage, and are having more contacts with the increased number of whites now living in the north. In contrast to Eskimo-white relations in some isolated parts of the Canadian arctic, Alaskan government policy enables the Eskimo to handle most of their own village affairs with little outside interference, though not necessarily with the unqualified respect of the whites.

Lack of severe village factionalism also contributes to the potential effectiveness of the Eskimo leader. The value placed on cooperation combined with the repression of aggression reduces the possiblitity of overt factionalism between generations—a common type of conflict found among peoples undergoing rapid change. Just as parents allow their teen-age children a large measure of freedom, so too do the older Eskimo pass on to young adults what was their traditional right to leadership positions. This pattern is particularly in evidence in organizations like the village councils and National Guard units, where the average age of the participants has decreased steadily in recent years.

One of the most difficult problems facing the new village leader is that of coordinating community action, for example, village clean up. Not only must the leader contend with lack of precedent, but he must be careful not to identify himself too closely with his white counterparts for fear that the other community members will believe he no longer is representing their needs and interests. The leader who ceases to share the norms, objectives, and aspirations of the group ceases to be a leader. Nor may he be authoritarian or aggressive in his actions for this goes directly against Eskimo values.

An illustration of how these three factors resulted in the loss of a capable village leader at Point Hope is the case of the "community electric power plant." Although a large majority of the community members were in favor of obtaining a local power plant, they had little experience or knowledge of how to implement such a plan. Nevertheless, with the planning and urging of the village council president, arrangements were made and the plant constructed. Problems arose immediately, most of them concerned with the amount of the monthly payment each family should make for electricity. Locally designated "bill collectors" refused to press for the payment of bills, at which point the council president, faced with the possibility of bankruptcy, aggressively reminded the villagers of what happens to white Americans who refuse to pay their bills. Although the installation of meters eventually resolved the financial problem, the leader lost much of his influence and was not re-elected to the council.

One of the most significant recent developments in north Alaska has been the emergence of the annual *Innupiak* conferences, in which Eskimo leaders from northern villages come together to discuss common problems. Meeting first at Barrow in 1962, and then at Kotzebue and Fairbanks in 1963 and 1964, they have discussed the possible revision of the duck hunting laws, the improvement of welfare and education programs, and matters of similar interest. A problem of immediate concern has to do with the question of land rights. Many villages have been surveyed and lots may soon be offered to Eskimo with the stipulation that they give up possible claim to other land in the region. Whatever feelings the Eskimo have on this issue may be effectively expressed through the medium of the *Innupiak* conferences.

Law and Social Control

The aboriginal Eskimo had few organizational ties outside his kin group, the two major ones being the hunting partners and the whaling crew—*karigi* memberships. Even here, hunting partners usually assumed the status of quasi-kin, and crew members unrelated to the *umialik* frequently changed affiliation, depending on the latter's skill, wealth, and luck in obtaining whales. These circumstances severely limited Eskimo social organization, and settlements and villages represented a community of interest rather than a corporate unit. Since there was no political organization, social sanctions, customary law, common goals, and norms provided the essential fabric of village structure (see Spencer 1959:444). The individual had great freedom of choice in his actions, but his security lay in cooperating and sharing with others.

Nonconforming individuals, such as an aggressive bully or persistent wife stealer, presented a continual problem in these settlements. If the nonconformist could not be curbed by the actions of kin or the force of public opinion, the one remaining alternative was to exclude him from participation in the community's economic and social life, a rather effective sanction given the unpredictable conditions of arctic life. If severe interpersonal conflicts arose between one or more members of different kin groups, the villagers were faced with a serious dilemma, for there was no available technique for resolving blood feuds once they had begun. It was not until the government assigned United States marshals to police this northern area that interfamily feuds disappeared entirely.

As long as the Eskimo's economic and social security depends on the assistance and support of others, gossip, ridicule, and ostracism can be quite effective in ensuring conformity to group norms. Eskimo socialization, emphasizing as it does rapid fulfillment of the child's needs and wants, freedom of action in many spheres, early participation in adultlike responsibilities with appropriate recognition for achievement, and the rejection of violence in any form, also encourages the formation of a conforming, rather than a rebellious, personality type.

This method of social control is weakened considerably, however, when family groups become less cohesive, when there is greater economic independence, and when conflicts in value orientations appear between generations. All of these trends have become quite apparent in recent years.

Temporarily broken homes were a major concern in the 1950s when the United States Public Health Service undertook a major campaign to reduce the incidence of active tuberculosis in Alaskan villages. The impact of this campaign was perhaps most pronounced at Kaktovik, where approximately 25 percent of the population were hospitalized for periods of up to two years. Of these, 6 percent were parents. Admission rates were strikingly high in other villages, requiring in each instance a pronounced family readjustment. Fortunately, recent advances in drug therapy now allow most tuberculosis patients to be treated in their own villages.

Family life also has suffered as a result of other factors: fathers and sons have left their communities for jobs in major employment centers; sons and daughters have been sent away to boarding schools; there has been a rapid increase of heavy drinking in the village and home. The latter problem is of such magnitude that it is a common topic of conversation in church, at village council meetings, and at informal gatherings.

Given these changes, it is hardly surprising that the traditional mechanisms of social control are losing some of their effectiveness. As adults become less dependent on others, they are less bound by public opinion. A long-term Eskimo employee of the DEW Line expressed his feelings on the matter: "No one's going to tell me not to have a drink. I've got a steady paying job and I can do what I want." Some of the highly acculturated young people offer similar opinions. After a short visit to Wainwright, a Barrow teen-ager spoke of the strict curfew in effect there.

> When I visited the village, I didn't know about the midnight curfew for young people. I went out until about three in the morning with a local girl. I went out again late the next night and on the following day a council member spoke to me at the post office about the curfew. I told him I was a visitor from Barrow and I shouldn't have to obey the curfew. He said I did, but I kept going out late anyway. Finally, the whole council called me in and told me I could not go out after twelve o'clock any more, and I said, "This is America, not Russia and I can go out as much as I like." The council didn't like that, but there was nothing they could do. I left soon afterwards, though. That Wainwright is a strict place.

After a similar visit to Kaktovik, this same youth gave further insight into his negative attitude toward the more isolated Eskimo villages:

After living in the States, I can't stand this place for very long. The people here, they don't know what it is like outside. Some of the boys brag about how good they are, but I just keep quiet, laughing inside. They haven't seen anything like I have. And another thing they don't have any respect for privacy. Why, they just come into your house without being invited and drink your coffee, or anything. The people at Barrow don't do things like that, they have much better manners and aren't so backward.

While these remarks represent an extreme position, many of the acculturated youth show little regard for the old Eskimo ways, and after leaving home, they simply ignore traditional pressures to conform. If their actions consistently disrupt village life, as in the case of individuals who become aggressive after drinking, they may be brought before a village council. The effectiveness of the council as a deterrent depends largely on the prestige of the councilors, their previous experience, the type of problem brought before them, and the degree of support given by local whites.

A few village councils were organized as early as the 1920s when they were encouraged by resident missionaries and teachers, but at best they were only nominally effective. The major impetus for the development of local self-government came in the mid-1930s when governmental responsibility for the Eskimo was placed under the jurisdiction of the Bureau of Indian Affairs. With the passing of the Indian Reorganization Act, Eskimo obtained the right to draft village constitutions and bylaws, ratify them by a majority vote, and submit them for approval to the Secretary of the Interior. Today, all Alaskan Eskimo villages with a population of 100 or more have some form of self-government. Most are organized formally with an elected president, vice-president, secretary, treasurer, and several councilors. They meet at regular intervals and take action on such common problems as supervising the operation of native cooperative stores, undertaking spring village clean-up campaigns, promoting civic improvements, and making and enforcing local regulations.

It is in the area of law enforcement that the councils face their greatest dilemma. Having established regulations against the importation of intoxicating beverages, the members have no way to enforce their ruling. The same problem occurs with regard to gambling, curfews, and the confinement of dogs. With the exception of Barrow, no community has obtained sufficient funds to hire a law enforcement officer and few local whites, even if requested to, wish to become involved in such a responsibility.

When an individual disregards a local regulation, he usually is approached by the president or another council member, reminded of the ruling, and told to conform. If he persists, he is brought before the council and asked to account for his behavior. This practice is most effective with village youth, but is pursued with adults as well. Occasionally, council members take direct action against young people for minor infractions; they may confiscate air rifles or slingshots used within village limits, or assign punitive tasks.

For more serious offences like minor theft, a combination of council and family pressures may be applied to the offender, who is usually a child or teen-ager. Until recently, theft was almost unheard of among the Eskimo, and adults still speak of this misdemeanor with strong feelings of indignation. In most northern coastal villages, though, the problem is of sufficient concern so that most householders have placed locks on their doors, which they use when going away for any length of time.

The problems which council members feel least able to resolve are those of drinking and the curfew. Although all liquor is forbidden by local ordinance, the moderate drinker seldom is criticized as long as he indulges in the quiet of his own home. Beer and alcohol are obtained by mail from Fairbanks, from a resident white, or from a friend recently returned from the "outside." Drinking is considered a problem when it results in such open hostility as wife beating or picking a fight. There also have been instances in the past few years of young Eskimo who, under the influence of liquor, kill the lead dog of another hunter, destroy furniture and other household items, or break into government buildings to steal. Generally, the forces of public opinion simply were not adequate to ensure future control of the offender. The problem is most serious at Barrow village. According to a middle-aged Eskimo:

> When I got back to Barrow from the Army in 1946, there was almost no drinking going on there. But now there is quite a lot. Eskimo go crazy when they drink. They just don't know how to hold their liquor. Kaktovik, for example, is a much smaller village and there is more control over the people. There, if someone is drinking too much, he is brought up before the council and told to stop. This is done in full view of the whole village. At Barrow, this isn't anywhere near as effective. There are too many people here who just don't care.

Most teen-agers and many children ignore curfews, and few parents are inclined to assist in enforcing this regulation. The young people are well aware that the council has little or no legal power to enforce its ruling, and therefore they disregard prohibitions unpleasant to them. In an attempt to combat this problem, Wainwright recently has tried to raise sufficient money through household assessments to incorporate the village, and thus give more legal status to the council's rulings.

Sexual offences occasionally are brought to the attention of a village council, as in the case of a fifty-year-old Eskimo man who was regularly having sexual relations with two young teen-agers, providing them with candy for their services. All three participants were taken before the local council and asked to confess. The confessions came easily but none of the parties showed any sign of remorse. The council eventually decided to inform the territorial police and the man was sent to the Nome jail for six months, an experience he thoroughly enjoyed. The girls were returned to their parents with the admonition to behave themselves in the future.

With sufficient complaint, a council may take action in marital conflicts. In one instance, a married man well known for his heavy drinking was brought before his village council for having sexual relations with another woman. Although he confessed, he refused to discontinue the arrangement, whereupon the council informed him he had to leave the village. He did leave, taking his family with him, but he returned alone several years later.

Although problems of deviation and social control exist, the large majority of Eskimo maintain a common set of standards covering a wide range of behavior and, with relatively few exceptions, actively conform to these standards. There is no sense of lawlessness, no rampant vandalism, delinquency, crime, sexual misconduct, or alcholism. The problems of social control that do appear are similar to those of any region undergoing rapid modernization. If, in the future, generational differences of what constitutes right and wrong become sharply drawn resulting in a highly relative definition of normative behavior, the problem of social control will become more serious. At present, the Eskimo are dealing as best they can with the organizational and cultural skills at their disposal. Only for serious offences do they turn to the outsider for assistance. The opportunity to develop local self-government using local initiative gives the Eskimo of this region an advantage not always found among peoples undergoing rapid modernization.

5

Cultural Values

MAN IS NOTED for his ability to adapt to his varied surroundings. This inherent flexibility also has enabled him to select given courses of action from a wide range of alternatives, the extent of choice being largely dependent upon the technological and environmental potential available to him. Within these limits, the range of choice is influenced strongly by the existing social structure and prevailing system of values. Having become familiar with the environment, technology, and social structure of the Eskimo, it is appropriate that we focus attention on the value system.

Values may be viewed as affectively charged ideas influencing alternative courses of action. Through the analysis of values it is possible to learn a great deal about how individuals or groups define their world, express their feelings, and make their judgments. In studying values, we are interested particularly in determining what alternative forms of behavior are available to the Eskimo and what motivates them to choose one over another. Verbal expressions that connote feelings and emotions also tell us much about values, whether they are directed toward an interest or goal, or are a response to some action that is positively or negatively sanctioned.

Due to the environmental and technological limitations previously discussed, most Eskimo settlements were, until recently, small, relatively isolated, and culturally homogeneous. Since the Eskimo had to devote most of their energies to gaining a living, variations in thought and behavior were largely directed toward experimentation which might better satisfy external demands. In the traditional context, the individual's desires closely paralleled the cultural definition of the desirable. Because they had little knowledge of Western technology and culture, the Eskimo's ideas of necessity and possibility were closely intertwined.

In spite of the homogeneity of traditional values, adequate description of these values is still difficult because of the Eskimo's culturally prescribed tendency to keep one's thoughts and feelings to oneself. Commenting on this attitude, the anthropologist Spencer has written of the north Alaskan Eskimo: "No one could feel free to indicate to others that he might be out of sorts. This was true in all interpersonal relationships. People talked, and still do so, of the weather, hunting, food. There was no attempt to evaluate situations or to pass judgement on them." (1959:249)

In some contexts this attitude still exists: Eskimo often underplay or conceal their unhappy states of mind. Nor do they appear to pay much overt attention to another's problems, not because they are unaware of them, but because it is tactful not to notice. They are, nevertheless, very sensitive to those feelings of others that are expressed. It is the lack of expression of feelings (but not of sensitivity), coupled with limited choice of alternatives throughout most of the Eskimo's history, that make the task of analyzing values difficult, a fact no doubt contributing to the minimal literature on the topic.

Man's Relation to Nature

A missionary trained in linguistics recently spent several years in north Alaska studying the Eskimo language. In the course of his investigations he noted continual use of the word "if" rather than "when" with reference to the future. The Eskimo language does not provide a choice between "if" or "when-in-the-future." With some frustration the missionary regularly heard the phrase "when Jesus comes" translated into Eskimo as "Jesus *kaitpan*," meaning "if Jesus comes."

Given the physical and social conditions in which they live, the Eskimo are quite aware of the tentativeness of life, the constant presence of unforeseen contingencies, and the lack of control over matters pertaining to subsistence and health. It is not surprising that one frequently hears other qualifying expressions such as "maybe," in regard to the future, or "we're all right so far" in response to an inquiry as to the health of a family. Even more explicit reference to life's tentativeness is contained in the common expression, "if I'm still alive," when commenting about some future action.

In each of these instances, the Eskimo reflects in his patterns of speech his fatalistic outlook on the world. It is not the fatalism of resignation, of "giving up" in the face of difficulty, but rather the realization that one has little control over the natural course of events. To a white outsider who sees the forces of nature as something to be controlled, this value can be quite disturbing. Commenting on Eskimo attitudes toward life and death, a public health nurse assigned to Alaska's northern region once said:

I am always surprised to see their easy acceptance of death. On many occasions, I have visited Eskimo villages to find that I arrived too late;

that a child had died a day or two before. The usual response to this was, "nurse arrived too late and the child died." There was never any thought, "if only she had come earlier," but a simple acceptance of fate.

We already know that the traditional Eskimo had a very limited knowledge of medicine, and that emphasis was placed on keeping well rather than getting well. Under these conditions, the people had few illusions regarding their ability to cure serious illnesses—other than through the services of a shaman. Even today, many of the village "health teams" are only minimally effective in implementing new sanitation and other health programs, largely because of the lack of support of older, less acculturated residents.

A fatalistic view of the world was given further support through traditional religious beliefs. Although an individual could attempt to exert influence over supernatural spirits by means of magic or ritual, or by following designated taboos, most Eskimo considered themselves to be at the mercy of hostile forces. The power contained in songs, charms, and names gave some feeling of control over the supernatural, particularly when used by a shaman, but even this assumed power often proved incapable of producing the desired result.

Fatalism is still a characteristic mode of response in many situations, but it is not accompanied by lassitude. On the contrary, hard work and industriousness are considered prime virtues. In every village adults are active much of the time, butchering meat, repairing fish nets, mending clothing, painting houses, improving ice cellars. Those adults who regularly rise late or in other ways give the impression of having little to do will be admonished by kin with, "How do you ever get your work done?" Being lazy is actively condemned for children and adults. Every village contains those families that do not like to hunt, are on relief, or cannot keep a job. When kin find that they are giving far more assistance than they receive, they exert informal pressure to equalize the exchange.

Hard work is not thought of as an end in itself, however, as is common among middle-class whites; nor is there any guiding principle that one should "work first and play later." Work and relaxation are both important and a person should not indulge in one too long without the other. The coffee break has become a highly popular part of any work gathering, even where there is pressure to finish a task as in the case of butchering meat. While there are jobs requiring immediate attention, such as storing meat in ice cellars to keep it from spoiling, or following the trail of game, most work is viewed casually, without any feeling that it must be completed at a given time. A girl hanging up laundry may stop half way through and turn to some other activity and perhaps not return until the following day. A young man may paint part of his bedroom wall and then take a nap.

This lack of emphasis on finishing a job for the sake of its immediate completion occasionally presents a problem for Eskimo employed by whites. Both whites and highly acculturated Eskimo have been known to make the generalized statement, "Eskimo have to learn to finish what they start," not taking into account that the Eskimo have a clear sense of job completion. What differs is the work situation in which the concept applies. Eskimo realize that boats need to be secured before a storm, that sufficient driftwood or other fuel must be stored for winter, and that wounded game should be tracked down and killed. But they may see no need to fill up the gas tank of a jeep at the end of the day, or automatically rewind a movie film or recording tape after using it.

Fatalism also is tempered by the value placed on self-reliance. Given the severity of the arctic environment and the limited food supply, this value always has had an important integrative function—the ability to take care of oneself, serving as a necessary prerequisite for survival. This is seen in the Eskimo's attitude toward physical illness. Only with the greatest reluctance is the individual willing to pass on his daily responsibilities temporarily to another. An Eskimo with an illness considered quite debilitating in Western society is far more likely to continue his or her work without complaint. This acceptance of illness as a normal part of the life cycle has its roots in the traditional culture pattern where attitudes of patience and endurance, as well as fatalism, were basic to the process of survival.

Actually, the man who works steadily at whatever task is before him, keeps his hunting and other equipment in good repair, and maintains an accurate account of the available food and other necessities of life, is not only being self-reliant; he is also exerting greater control over the world around him and thereby leaving less to fate.

Man's Relation with Man

Nobody ever tells an Eskimo what to do. But some people are smarter than others and can give good advice. They are the leaders.

We always try to help each other, that is the best way. Everybody works together, but if you don't do the right things, then people won't help you.

There has always been a strong current of individualism flowing through Eskimo culture, although seldom is it so marked as to lead to open conflict or isolation of the person. It is seen in the permissiveness of child rearing which stresses respect for the thoughts and feelings of the young. The way in which a man provides for his wife and children is largely an individual responsibility. The wife, too, is free to make many decisions such as whether or not she will accompany her husband on a long hunting trip or visit relatives in another village. Prestige is more commonly gained through individual achievements than through association in a particular group.

Aboriginally, man's relation with the supernatural was viewed as a personal struggle, and the shaman gained his power through highly personal experiences rather than in the context of group ritual. Nor did the *umialik* have any clearly defined authority over others, for his role as leader was determined by his own personal qualities and skills. Except within the family, orders and commands were not expected from others and the authoritarian bully met great resentment. Most interpersonal conflicts were settled man to man with little or no outside mediation. Decision making between families was, and still is, undertaken in a spirit of informal consultation. Only rarely did a dominant village leader speak out authoritatively on behalf of those to whom he was not related by kin, and in such instances there was no assurance that his decisions would be carried out.

A recognized sense of competition further highlighted the value placed on individualism, for most rivalry took place between individuals rather than groups. Whaling crews and *karigi* members seldom competed against one another and intervillage rivalry was limited to generous gift-giving exploits at the annual Messenger Feasts. However, the spirit of individual competition always has assumed some importance.

Many Eskimo sports and games continually matched one man against another as in foot, boat, and dog races, tests of strength, song duels, dancing, and storytelling. Ingenuity was tested by one's ability to invent new stories and games. Even kickball, a team effort, featured individual control of the ball. There was betting on which of the good hunters would obtain the largest number of seals in a given season. Competitions were held to determine who could make the best harpoon, kayak, and other material objects. Women competed in skin sewing, making clothing, making baskets, and the like.

This type of competition is common today and as such provides a continuing reminder of the need to perform well. Not only may physical survival someday depend upon it, but feelings of competitiveness in the exhibition of skills motivates others to do even better and often leads to new and improved techniques. This attribute functions equally well in a Western context for one of the qualities highly admired by whites is the Eskimo's ingenuity in using available resources to solve technical problems. Their personal initiative gained from a sense of competition is internally consistent with other Eskimo values of self-reliance, self-confidence, and generosity. In the past the lavish giftgiving of the Messenger Feast gave personal status, but it also served as a reminder of the importance of sharing.

There are several techniques that keep competition from becoming too disruptive socially. Rivalry is expected to be of the good-natured kind, never psychologically injurious to any specific person. Modesty being an important virtue, one should not flaunt one's skills in the face of another or recount one's achievements in a boasting manner. This is not a self-effacing type of modesty, but one that allows people to admit their own merits in a matter-of-fact tone as in "I make good mukluks." Pseudo-self-effacement is occasionally used to draw attention to oneself. A good hunter, who has returned from a trip with an unusually large supply of meat, might remark, "Oh it is nothing, anybody could have done it."

Before the introduction of Christianity, shamans served as a check on the seemingly "too successful" man. The hunter who always got his kill or always appeared able to accomplish any task to which he set himself soon incurred the displeasure of the shaman. If he boasted about his performance or threatened the shaman's own position of leadership, the latter would use his traditional techniques to plot the successful man's downfall. Sanctions such as these had the cultural effect of assuring a certain uniformity of status which paved the way for the expression of another dominant value, that of cooperation and reciprocal exchange.

The idea of cooperation was instilled in the child at a young age. In the earliest years the infant was preoccupied with gratifying his own wants and developing skills to manipulate his surroundings. As he became older, he soon learned that his needs were more likely to be fulfilled when he gave assistance around the house, tended a younger brother or sister, or carried driftwood home to be stored. If he refused to assist or was "lazy," he soon incurred the disfavor of those on whom he was most dependent— his parents, older siblings, and other extended kin. Expectations of cooperation were less apparent among quasi-kin or members of unrelated families.

In addition, the child was encouraged to emulate those older than himself in such a way that they became for him important symbols of identification. Girls learned from older sisters and mothers the performance of skin sewing, meat butchering, making clothes, and numerous household chores. Boys learned how to hunt, prepare skins, make kayaks, and carry out similar masculine endeavors. Children soon learned that family members were highly dependent upon each other for many of their comforts and conveniences in daily life. By the time a child had reached his teens he usually had developed sufficient empathy with close kin to realize that their wishes and needs were important to take into account as well as his own. Achieving manhood, the adult continued to maintain a strong sense of identification with members of his own kin group and as such, was more likely to subordinate his own personal interests to the welfare of the group. To those with whom he identified less, that is, quasi-kin, hunting and joking partners, and other village residents in that order, he was more likely to act in terms of their accommodation to his expectations and needs. Given these conditions, it is easy to understand why the "poorest" Eskimo was defined as the person without kin, the individual who had no one to turn to in time of need. Economic and social security were largely drawn from the extended family, where the giving and receiving of assistance was expected as a matter of course.

If cooperation is still an important ideal in many families, the opportunity for its active expression is becoming more limited due to the increased geographical mobility of many village residents. In those families where traditional economic pursuits are followed, expectations regarding labor exchange, borrowing, and sharing usually are realized. Men hunt together, sharing their catch. Women assist one another with baby tending, carrying water, and similar household responsibilities. Members of related families help each other constructing, repairing, and painting houses, borrow each other's boats, sleds, and dogs, and share the use of generators, washing machines, and other equipment. However, many men, and occasionally women, leave their communities for seasonal or year-round employment elsewhere.

Seasonal migration is very evident at Point Hope. Men leave home for summer jobs as soon as seal hunting is over in early June. They seek jobs as miners in Nome, as construction workers in Fairbanks, Anchorage, and Kotzebue, or at one of the many military sites scattered throughout northern and central Alaska. Most men are hired as wage laborers. A few have become skilled in carpentry, mechanics, and other construction trades. Those belonging to a union may find summer jobs through the employment office in Fairbanks, thus enabling them to leave directly for the work site.

Whatever the position, men soon find that their success on the job depends largely on individual rather than cooperative effort and, as such, conflicts with much of their past experience and cultural outlook. Those who work "outside" are expected to send most of their salary home, an arrangement that is upheld by older married men far more often than by the young single adults (see VanStone 1960).

In Point Hope and other Eskimo villages many men have been able to combine successfully seasonal wage employment in the summer with aboriginal subsistence activities at other times of the year, since their outside employment comes at a time when there is relatively little to do in their villages. Nevertheless, seasonal absence of the male head of the family does weaken family attachments and those with related kin. The younger men gain economic independence working away from home, which limits their ability to learn traditional subsistence techniques, reduces parental authority, and sets them apart socially.

In other villages like Barrow and Kaktovik jobs are available locally, but even here, the nature of the work leaves men little time to engage in traditionally cooperative activities. Working a six-day week, few individuals can give more than minimal assistance to others and therefore can expect little in return. With sufficient cash income to purchase most of their food and other required goods, it would be possible to share these items with the full-time hunter in exchange for fresh meat, fish, and other traditional products. Yet, this modern version of reciprocal exchange is unusual, and the transaction more often occurs through the medium of the native village store.

Many Eskimo express concern over this turn of events, on the one hand wanting the material advantages of a good cash income, but on the other, disliking the penalty they must pay. Those who are uncooperative, without apparent justification, come in for their share of criticism from those who are more tradition oriented. "That family always push for themselves," was said of a couple who remained aloof from their kin. An older man who did little for others was rumored to have made his daughter pay board for her small son when the latter stayed overnight. A coffee-shop owner was criticized for not taking care of her children, "because she was only interested in making money feeding the young people."

As the importance of the extended family continues to decline, we may expect a further reduction of the traditional patterns of cooperation. The question of whether this value can be transplanted to the community at large depends on the root of the Eskimo's cultural identification and his newly formed goals. The one village institution that consistently has had real meaning for the Eskimo is the Christian church. Here, members contribute freely of their time and energy to repair and maintain the buildings and other facilities. Schools and post offices also are considered vital community institutions. Because of its small size, Kaktovik was without these facilities for many years. After numerous requests to the government had gone unheeded, the local residents obtained sufficient materials from a nearby military site and together constructed their own school and post office buildings. Recent United States congressional action now has provided appropriations enabling Eskimo villages to undertake their own "self-help" village projects, and it will be interesting to learn the extent to which the Eskimo of this region make use of these funds. The future of these communities will be determined in part by the members' ability to readapt their cooperative patterns to fit the modern context.

Values and Personality

When a person is motivated to do what is culturally defined as desirable, when his own values are similar to those of the culture of which he is a part, then cultural values and personality traits are as identical as they ever can be. However, when individuals are unable to fulfill culturally approved goals, or are inclined to fulfill culturally unapproved goals, conflicts arise which often develop into characteristic reactions. Attempts at accommodation to these internal stresses may be culturally approved or disapproved, healthy or neurotic, but in either instance, they frequently become a subconscious part of the personality (Lantis 1959).

A good illustration of this process is seen in the Eskimo's repression of aggression. From an early age, the child is encouraged to be friendly, open, genial, warm, and outgoing. White visitors to the arctic generally comment upon the frequent smile on the face of the Eskimo child. Although the child occasionally masks hostile feelings, he learns early that a friendly approach to others brings high rewards in the way of affection and praise. "That boy is even tempered, he never gets mad at anybody" is a common statement of praise. Warm personal attachments give a kind of social and psychological security that further adds to the desire to be friendly.

The aggressive child, on the other hand, is condemned as being "unfriendly." The Alaskan Indian is pointed out as an example: "They not friendly. They walk with fists (doubled up) all the time." Young bullies with strong tempers are characteristically subjects for gossip.

This type of upbringing is little preparation for facing the many conflicts and frustrations of adult life. The Eskimo youth is expected to be self-reliant in a physical and supernatural world over which he has little control. He must be friendly even with those people he may dislike. He should maintain a sense of pride but remain modest, be prepared for action but have patience. We may assume that these long-continued frustrations build up impulses toward agression in the individual. Since others strongly condemn any overt expression of these feelings, the individual simply suppresses them (that is, they seldom come to his conscious awareness) except during sudden seemingly unexplainable outbursts of temper during which a mother shouts at her children, or a man beats his wife or destroys someone's property. On rare occasions today, but more frequently in the past, these severe outbursts resulted in murder—or when turned inward, suicide.

Though physical aggression is disapproved of, there are a number of other outlets into which these feelings may be channeled. Verbal aggression takes the form of gossip. When the object of aggression is a white man or group, hostility may be expressed more openly in "hate" talk and fantasies of vengeance. Another way of expressing hostility toward non-Eskimo is to talk about them in their presence, in the Eskimo language. This is one of the major uses that Eskimo teen-agers see in their language today, although the practice is not limited to them. People seem to fear even a suggestion of verbal hostility, so that individuals are never left to determine for themselves whether a personal remark is a joke or not. The speaker invariably makes his harmless intention explicit by saying, "I jokes." This pattern, too, is true of all age groups.

Another acceptable way of expressing hostility is by not speaking to the offender. If people become sufficiently angry they may not speak to one another for several weeks or even months. When sharply criticized, an Eskimo may simply leave the room or area without saying a word and not return until he feels that the critic has calmed down. If one cannot avoid a hostile situation, then it is best to leave. In the past whole communities have moved in order to avoid a conflict of major proportions; the most recent example occurred in Greenland, when the Thule Eskimo relocated themselves following a conflict with a recently established United States Air Force base.

The image the Eskimo presents to others is one of sociability and resourcefulness. Not infrequently, however, his private image of himself contains feelings of loneliness and/or inadequacy. An Eskimo usually tries to surround himself with familiar, friendly people. Rarely does a youth or adult entertain himself alone, preferring the company of others. Under the conditions of high individual and family mobility described previously, people often complain of feeling lonely. Darkness is "lonely." "Loneliness" is a synonym for boredom. A person living in a house alone must be lonely. Attachment to one's home is strong and when teen-agers go away to boarding schools, they often become extremely lonely and homesick. A person who likes to be alone is viewed with suspicion and distrust. Individuals seen alone in an open boat or on the tundra are rumored to be Indians or spies.

Feelings of inadequacy, too, are becoming more evident in recent years, particularly in those villages undergoing rapid Westernization. In Kaktovik, for example, many middle-aged women indicated strong feelings of inadequacy in response to a psychological questionnaire administered by the author. These women had had less contact with the Western world than either their husbands, many of whom work steadily at a nearby radar site, or their children, who attend school locally or farther south. As a consequence, the women felt socially isolated from many of the changes going on around them. Furthermore, some of their traditional mechanisms for gaining prestige and contributing to family support, such as skin sewing, had diminished without adequate replacement. Under these changing conditions, many middle-aged women felt insecure and inadequate, yet these feelings did not lead to the expressions of anxiety that we would expect to find in Western society. The Eskimo repress feelings of anxiety because they conflict with the high value placed on self-reliance and resourcefulness in much the same way that aggression conflicts with the values of friendliness and cooperation. Instead, the questionnaire results suggested that feelings of anxiety were inverted and appeared as symptoms of inner tension (see Chance 1962).

To date, Eskimo men show few symptoms of personality difficulty or malfunctioning. The reasons for this successful psychological adjustment and the chances for its continuance in the future will be discussed in the following chapter.

6

The Dynamics of Change

I N THE FIRST CHAPTER we traced the history of the north Alaskan Eskimo and saw some of the ways in which they have been influenced by
Western civilization. The arrival of whalers in the 1850s, followed
by traders, missionaries, school teachers, doctors, nurses, construction workers, and military personnel, has contributed to the Eskimo's growing awareness of modern American technology and society. For many years the
changes brought about by this knowledge were relatively slow, resulting in
gradual modification of the traditional native culture. This was largely due
to the fact that the newcomers had to adapt their way of life to that of
the Eskimo; in the early contact period the adjustment problems were more
the concern of the former than of the latter.

More recently, however, this situation has undergone an almost complete reversal. Increased contact with whites has led many Eskimo to
adopt numerous material and social traits of Western society. They purchase large quantities of Western goods and services, build multiroom houses,
wear suits, dresses, and other Western-styled clothing, participate in Western games, dances, religious and secular holiday activities. At the same
time, interest in traditional Eskimo activities such as hunting and fishing,
traditional games and dances, skin sewing, and native craftsmanship has
lessened and in some instances disappeared. Although this pattern varies
among individuals at different times and places, it is quite clear that the
contemporary Eskimo tend to identify themselves more and more with
Western society and culture, discarding in the process much of their ethnic
heritage. As the anthropologist Margaret Lantis has stated: "Eskimos are
trying just as hard today to adapt as they did 500 or 900 years ago; the
difficulty is that they are adapting not to the Arctic but to the Temperate
Zone way of living. The new people with their new standards have nearly
overwhelmed the Eskimos, not in numbers but in wishes and wants."

(Lantis 1958:126) This pattern is particularly pronounced among the teenage youth, but it is also clearly evident among many members of the older generations.

What are the implications of this pattern for the future of the Eskimo? Are the newly acquired goals and values capable of realization or will they eventually lead to social and psychological frustration, conflict, and disorganization? In determining the answers to these questions it is necessary to look at the effects of these changes on community integration, that is, the ability of the community members to adapt and still maintain their basic institutions intact; on the social and cultural barriers and stimulants to change; on problems of cultural identity, and other significant factors influencing the dynamics of change among the Eskimo.

These remarks point out another important feature of anthropological investigation. Until now, our concern has been largely that of presenting a descriptive picture of Eskimo life. Yet anthropologists usually gather and interpret their field data with certain theoretical issues in mind. In this chapter, the reader will learn how an anthropologist organizes his data around a conceptual scheme with which he is particularly interested, develops hypotheses, tests them through the use of analytical classifications, and presents his findings. In this way, the reader can gain some understanding of how the anthropologist thinks and works as well as of the people he is describing.

Changes in Village Integration

In today's world, cultures are constantly changing. The rate may be minimal, due perhaps to cultural "drift"; or it may be maximal, as when the members of one society completely assimilate the members of another; but it is never static. There is a tendency to assume that when changes occur with great rapidity and encompass a large segment of the population, severe disruption results, whereas when changes are slow or cautious, such disturbance is less likely to occur. Indeed, a brief survey of the literature strongly supports this assumption, and it is particularly evident where small nonliterate societies have come into extensive contact with members of Western civilization. Following initial confrontation, conflict in roles and values, drastic ecological and demographic shifts, changing levels of aspiration, and use of coercion and force by the dominant group to attain its objectives are but a few of the many conditions predisposing to acculturative conflict and disorganization.

There have been occasions, however, when acculturation has proceeded with relatively little turmoil, and the subordinate group has been able to make a positive adjustment to the impact of the dominant society (see Chance 1960). It was this interest in the factors that lead to positive social and psychological integration under conditions of rapid change that first drew the author to study the Eskimo. Having learned from anthropologists recently returned from north Alaska that the people there appeared to be adapting very well to extensive changes, he chose this area for the study.

The first village in which fieldwork was undertaken was Kaktovik, chosen because it had undergone the greatest amount of change in the shortest period of time.[1] Located on Barter Island along the arctic coast sixty miles from the Canadian boundary, this small village of a little over 100 inhabitants is one of the most geographically isolated villages in all of Alaska, and until recently its members had to rely on hunting and fishing as their major means of livelihood. While many of the residents grew up in this part of Alaska, they did not come together to form a permanent village until the late 1940s and early 1950s. Only when the United States Coast and Geodetic Survey and the military began hiring local Eskimo for surveying and unskilled construction work did Kaktovik become formally recognized as a community. Prior to this time, most of the Eskimo lived in small family clusters scattered along the northeast part of the Alaskan coast, and except for infrequent meetings with missionaries, bush pilots, and nearby traders, they had very little face-to-face contact with whites.

In 1953–1954 when construction began on the Barter Island radar installation, the world of the Kaktovik Eskimo underwent a dramatic change. The radar site was located within a few hundred yards of the newly emerging village, and all available Eskimo men were given employment at high salaries. Since there were not enough local residents to fill the new positions, a number of families moved to the village from other communities as far away as Wainwright and Aklavik. While some were newcomers, quite a few of these new immigrants were actually returning to an area in which they had lived earlier and they had many friends and relatives in the community. This influx of new residents was not large enough to disrupt seriously the close kin and friendship ties characteristic of most of the older community members.

During the period of construction, several Eskimo received specialized training in semiskilled occupations, and a few even achieved positions as union carpenters and mechanics. Eskimo and whites worked together, ate together in the mess hall, participated jointly in recreational activities such as volleyball and games of strength, and in other ways shared many occupational and social experiences. At the request of the lay Eskimo Presbyterian minister, an old building was donated by the DEW Line to serve as a chapel.

Although problems of drinking and sexual misconduct occasionally arose, the government policy enabling the Eskimo to set up their own restrictions concerning the admittance of whites to the village kept this potentially disruptive force under control. Those white men who made friends with the Eskimo and participated in their social and recreational

---

[1] The following account of the changes that have occurred in Kaktovik is largely drawn from two previously published articles (Chance 1960; 1965).

life were welcomed by the community members, and those who were viewed as a potential threat to the village were discouraged. Any man, white or Eskimo, causing serious problems in the village or at the site was fired or sent to another installation.

Positive interethnic relations also were furthered by the congruence of traditional Eskimo leadership traits and those required to articulate with whites. The Eskimo leaders' mental alertness, industriousness, generosity, cooperativeness, and ability to learn new technical skills were attributes valued highly by whites, which enabled the local leaders to maintain their effectiveness and position of importance in both groups. At Kaktovik, the two traditionally recognized leaders worked steadily as carpenters, machine operators, and labor foremen and at the same time formed close ties with construction and government personnel in the area.

In 1957, major construction of the DEW Line was completed. This did not result in a reduction of jobs, however, since extensive maintenance was required. During the summers approximately 75 percent of the men in the village still earn salaries of $600 a month. For most of these men this is a full-time, relatively permanent, occupation. Although unions ceased to function at the close of construction, and most salaries no longer differentiate between occupational skills, members of all age groups over eighteen continue to work at the site in preference to their earlier pattern of hunting, fishing, and trapping.

As might be expected, the changes that occurred in this short period of time were extensive. Traditional subsistence patterns were replaced by full-time wage work, requiring the residents to remain in the village throughout the year. Hunting and fishing became week-end activities for members of most families. Much of the necessary food and other staples were purchased in the local store or flown in from Fairbanks with the assistance of the military. The decrease in hunting limited the undertaking of other traditional activities such as skin sewing and making most native clothing and skin boats. Driftwood houses were replaced by those of Western design, with much of the materials coming from the military dump. Medical care became more easily available through the male nurse or doctor assigned to the radar site. Military chartered air service made it possible for the residents to fly to Barrow for serious illness or childbirth. These new services, plus a carefully protected water supply drawn from a nearby lake, enabled the local villagers to maintain a state of health far above that of most Eskimo.

In 1951, when a full-time native teacher was assigned to Kaktovik, the people achieved one of their principal goals. During the years following the teacher's arrival, strong interest in education and in learning the English language led some of the adults to attend classes along with their children. As might be expected, however, most older children soon exceeded their parents in knowledge of English as well as in number of grades completed.

When a post office was established a few years later, the Kaktovik people were finally able to order their own fresh foods, clothing, outboard motors, guns, and other items, directly from mail-order houses. In addition, the cooperative purchase of several large generators, flown in by mail plane, enabled every family to benefit from electric power. Along with lighting, the Eskimo obtained washing machines, radios, and record players. Many families purchased their own tape recorders which they used to send "tape letters" to friends and relatives at Barrow, Wainwright, Point Hope, and Fairbanks. Movies loaned by the DEW Line personnel were run off on the the church projector.

What were the effects of these tremendous changes on the people? The data gathered during the first phase of the study (1958) suggested that the many changes brought on by increased contact and new employment had not seriously affected the internal stability of the group. The whole community maintained warm interpersonal relations and high morale. Games, dances, song fests, and other recreational activities constantly brought people together for periods of fellowship and relaxation. During the first summer's fieldwork, the author regularly participated in the evening game of volleyball which usually included between 70 and 80 percent of the adolescent and adult village population.

In other community activities, such as the construction of the school, the post office, or the improvement of the church, or in the more day-to-day matters of helping carry water to the home, hauling a whaleboat up on the beach, or caring for a neighbor's children, there was frequent face-to-face contact. Although many changes occurred in the village, they appeared not to have disrupted the amount of interaction between the members. Because the Eskimo had moved from scattered homes along the coast to a permanent village, one could even speak of an increase in interaction.

Intravillage contacts were very important if the normative structure was to remain at all effective under conditions of rapid and extensive change. In Kaktovik, norms appeared to be both widely shared and clearly defined. While some cultural patterns had changed and others had been created to fit the new environmental and behavioral situation, these changes were effected without undue tension and stress. Many of the traditional patterns of behavior, such as those associated with sharing and cooperation, were strongly maintained. At the time of this phase of the field work hunting partnerships still were maintained. These partners characteristically shared with one another all the caribou, *ugrook,* beluga, and other large game that had been killed, leaving only the smaller game, like seal and duck, to be claimed individually. After a particularly successful hunt, meat was distributed to the many relatives of the hunters as well.

Norms regarding drinking, interpersonal relations, and religious behavior also were firmly held, which was not the case in some of the other villages situated along the Alaskan coast. Only once in the twelve years immediately prior to the study had these Eskimo to deal with a serious drinking problem involving a member of their own village. In this instance, after all other attempts at correction had failed, the community leaders finally told the individual concerned to either discontinue his excessive drinking or leave the village. Shortly thereafter, the man returned to his earlier home in Canada. Well-attended church services (80 to 90 percent of the population) provided the native minister with an excellent opportunity to extol the values of good Christian living, and the enthusiasm of the congregation, expressed in individual prayer offerings, hymn singing, and "public confessionals," reflected the level of community interest and general support of these religious views.

These illustrations give some indication of the positive adjustment the Kaktovik Eskimo were making to the rapid changes taking place at that time. Reasons for this relatively smooth adjustment appeared to be multiple.

Factors Influencing Positive Change

We may begin by considering the size and density of the population undergoing the change. Small compact villages like Kaktovik usually have a high rate of social interaction which offers maximum opportunity for intragroup communication. During periods of cultural stability, this opportunity need not be utilized fully, for traditional norms and values undergo little variation. But in situations of rapid and extensive change, positive adjustment does not occur unless the old norms that have become inoperative are adequately replaced by those appropriate to the new situation. At Kaktovik, the successful substitution of new norms was related directly to the high intensity of interaction and communication among the Eskimo. While this was not a sufficient condition for normative consensus, it was a necessary one.

Second, the traditional kinship system remained stable. Kin ties of either a primary or secondary sort bound together fifteen of the eighteen households. The practice of extending kinship privileges to nonkin by means of formal partnerships effectively integrated the three other household units as well. The whole village, therefore, was joined by this kin or quasi-kinship network. Any member faced with a potentially stressful situation had a definite set of individuals he could turn to for immediate support.

Third, most of the newly defined goals were realized successfully. Increased contact between whites and Eskimo had led to a much higher set of aspirations in the latter. These aspirations were formulated most explicitly in the desire for material goods—goods usually unattainable given the traditional economy of the average Eskimo. Furthermore, this desire was encouraged by traders, military personnel, white schoolteachers, and and others in direct contact with the native population. We may contrast this situation with the Aleut Eskimo community of Nikolski where Berreman found that:

> Behaviors, values, and goals shifted to those advocated by the school teacher and were associated with the new and foreign culture. The gravity of this situation is shown by the fact that in 1952 every child over nine years of age planned to emigrate from the community as soon as possible. Several have already gone. The reasons given invariably indicate a desire to be successful in the White man's way of life. (1954:106)

In contrast to Nikolski, the population of Kaktovik had doubled in a little over six years, and identification with the community became stronger rather than weaker. This was due in large part to the availability of a ready cash income which enabled the Eskimo to attain locally many of their newly defined goals. Most village residents were able to purchase gas generators, outboard motors, up-to-date hunting and fishing equipment, household furnishings, kitchen utensils, and many other material items that they desired. To the average Eskimo living at Kaktovik, life had suddenly become easier and more comfortable. Furthermore, the obtainment of basic physical needs like food and clothing had become more predictable. The year-round salary check resolved much of the anxiety facing every member of the family, who had previously wondered whether enough food was stored to last out the coming winter.

Fourth, the rapid changes that had taken place in the village did not limit the effectiveness of the traditional Eskimo leader. An assessment of the leadership patterns in the village indicated that behavior traditionally associated with the leadership role had been easily linked with behavior necessary to lead vis-à-vis the whites. By means of their friendly manner, mental alertness, and the ease with which they acquired new technical skills, traditionally acceptable leaders gained the white man's respect and admiration. The dominant village leadership actually was shared by two closely related men of good judgment and material wealth (by both traditional and Western standards), who were a major force in developing strong community spirit and identification. While the leadership criteria varied somewhat between the two groups, both recognized the same individuals as leaders.

Fifth, the Kaktovik Eskimo were able to maintain their autonomy within the context of an economic dependency due to the continuing policy of close cooperation and friendliness between DEW Line officials and Eskimo leaders.

The Kaktovik Eskimo had another advantage in that most government personnel looked upon them as a real asset. In discussing the decision to employ Eskimo at Point Barrow, Alaska, Commander Roberts of the United States Navy wrote:

The Eskimo of this area by disposition is light hearted and cheerful. He is generally peaceable and not easily discouraged. He has a keen sense of humor. He is trustworthy, honest and a hard-working man. It was, therefore, believed that no problem would arise in utilizing the Eskimo in positions where he was qualified, and to work hand-in-hand with men from other parts of the Territory of Alaska and from the United States. (1954:41)

Similar attitudes expressed by nearby DEW Line officials enabled the Eskimo to maintain a sense of pride and self-respect not just in terms of their own physical environment, but as a part of the larger Western society as well. Clearly, the ability to maintain one's self-respect was a vital consideration if Eskimo were to adjust to their rapidly changing world.

Finally, the fact that all men, regardless of age, had equal opportunity to receive salaried employment and participate in this new way of life resolved a potentially difficult problem frequently found in acculturation situations—where increased economic opportunities and advantages for the young result in loss of respect and prestige for the old. The disorganizing elements inherent in generational factionalism were not then evident in Kaktovik.

In summary, the key intervening factors affecting Kaktovik's successful adjustment appeared to be the following: first, the village was formed voluntarily in response to new employment opportunities made available by the military and other governmental personnel coming into the area. It brought together many related families previously scattered along the coast—and in so doing promoted increased communication, mutual cooperation, and village solidarity. The scarcity of personnel enabled any Eskimo male capable of passing a physical examination to have a high-salaried job. There was little or no economic competition for available positions. Steady income and allied services gave increased security in the satisfaction of basic physical needs such as food, clothing, and medical care and in related cultural "needs" such as those associated with the purchase of material goods and with feelings of self-esteem. Strong and stable leadership forestalled serious internal schisms and fostered favorable external relations with outsiders. This was aided by the congruence of aboriginal leadership traits and those required to articulate with whites. White policy encouraged good relations with Eskimo, retention of Eskimo leaders, and noninterference in Eskimo affairs. Finally, continued freedom of action enabled the Eskimo at all age levels to choose major patterns of life activity without outside coercion.

Regional Patterns of Change

Is Kaktovik unique in its relatively smooth adjustment to rapid change, or is this pattern also characteristic of other north Alaskan Eskimo villages? Actually, making a comparison is difficult because of important differences in type and extent of change in each community. At Point Hope, traditional subsistence activities fulfill most of the members' needs, but recently acquired wants require supplemental cash income. Since there are very few local opportunities for employment, most men seek summer jobs outside. The fact that there are not many resident whites keeps to a minimum village contacts with this group. How long this arrangement will continue depends on the extent of satisfactions derived from community life. In 1960, the anthropologist James VanStone wrote: "The Point Hopers, like most rural people everwhere, depend on their own small community for the satisfaction of their major wants. When the point is reached where residence in the village leaves too many wants unsatisfied, the community will begin to disintegrate." (1960:188) To date, continuing interest in traditional forms of subsistence and social life have effectively prevented this development.

At Wainwright, economic and social changes are even less accelerated, but for a different reason. Opportunities for local wage work are few and many Eskimo seek summer employment in other towns and cities. But a far larger number have left Wainwright permanently. Those aspiring to a Western mode of life have emigrated to Fairbanks, southern Alaska, or the "lower States." There is even a small enclave of Wainwright Eskimo ivory carvers living in Seattle, Washington. A study of Wainwright emigration patterns between World War II and 1962 indicated that almost 100 residents had left the community permanently. Children of these emigrants seldom return to the village, even when they have relatives living there.

Of those who now reside in the community, practically all engage in hunting and other traditional economic pursuits. Although not as well situated for whaling as Barrow, Wainwright families are nonetheless quite self-sufficient because of their large catches of seal, walrus, beluga, and caribou. Local contracts with whites are limited to resident schoolteachers, missionaries, visiting state and federal government officials, and the occasional scientist.

Relations between villagers and schoolteachers vary according to the personalities and social attributes of the latter. Some are well liked and enter easily into local affairs. Others may simply be ignored or laughed at behind their backs. In extreme cases of dislike, more dramatic action is taken, such as searching the teacher's trash for incriminating evidence of liquor or petitioning the Bureau of Indian Affairs for the person's removal.

Missionaries generally are accepted warmly and hospitably, with resentment shown only if a missionary is too aggressive or makes disparaging remarks about the other local church. Wainwright has had quite a few missionaries in recent years, and, during one month in the summer of 1962, five were in residence. In most instances, missionaries have far more day-to-day contact with the Eskimo than do the schoolteachers, and those who have learned the Eskimo language are particularly well received.

Visiting scientists affiliated with the Arctic Research Laboratory at Barrow and government officials often make brief visits to Wainwright, but their negotiations and contacts are usually limited to a few of the more acculturated Eskimo whose intellectual or commercial interests draw them to seek association with whites. In general, the more willing the white resident is to try Eskimo ways of living, speaking, dressing, and eating, and the more warm and generous he is, the more likely it is that the Eskimo will accept him.

Barrow village presents an entirely different picture, having a much larger population (over 1200), more opportunities for local wage work, and a large contingent of white military, government, and other administrative and service personnel. Following Spencer's study of the Barrow Eskimo in 1952–1953, he commented on the importance of the family in maintaining community integration: "'It would appear that only if the family system is disrupted will community disorganization on a large scale occur. For despite the cash income, the social organization of the aboriginal Eskimo is still a potent force." (1959:364) While the basic cooperative family is still a significant force for integration, the continuous swelling of Barrow's population has sorely tried the community leaders' efforts to deal with the social problems which now confront them.

Problems of delinquency and minor crimes have reached such proportions that, in 1962, a team of investigators from the Division of Youth and Adult Authority of the state Department of Health and Welfare went to Barrow to study the situation. Drinking and theft were particularly common among male youths and adults; drinking and sexual misdemeanors were common among girls and women. Most offences were committed by individuals rather than groups, although teen-age gangs were beginning to emerge. The investigators stressed the difficulty of obtaining capable and experienced community-wide leaders, the ineffective methods of social control, boredom, and the lack of social cohesion as key factors influencing the rising rate of delinquency and crime. While these problems are found in all Eskimo communities today, they are less serious in those of smaller size where family ties are stronger, leadership is more influential, and gossip and other traditional techniques of social control are more effective.

Barrow village faces an additional problem: the often strained relations between Eskimo and whites causes members of each ethnic group to live in their own separate worlds, largely ignoring the other. It is important not to overemphasize the negative quality of these relationships, nor to generalize to all Eskimo or whites, but this quality is nevertheless evident in many spheres.

In contrast to the past when whites had to adapt much of their way of life to that of the Eskimo, today the Barrow Eskimo is in many ways trying to adapt to the white world, with various consequences. One immediate effect of this change is a loss in prestige. As Western technology enables whites to erect their own artificial environment, less recognition is given to the Eskimo's ability to survive in his natural environment. This loss in prestige is furthered by the Eskimo's lack of occupational skills, which usually limits his employment to that of common labor. While a few Eskimo have been trained to assume positions as skilled mechanics, tractor operators, clerks, and scientific assistants, the majority must assume more menial responsibilities.

Poor Eskimo housing and sanitary facilities, as defined by Western standards, have had their effect on white attitudes toward the Eskimo. Not only are most native houses considered slum dwellings, but conditions within the homes seldom fit white working- or middle-class norms of cleanliness. Some of the most commonly expressed criticisms of the Eskimo reflect these differential attitudes toward housing, sanitation, and cleanliness.

Many middle-aged and older Eskimo have a limited knowledge of the English language and the outside world, which also contributes to white feelings of disparagement. The Eskimo often are inhibited in their conversations with whites except in those areas where they have extensive knowledge and experience. Unfortunately, these topics usually hold little interest for whites, which in turn adds to the Eskimo's sense of inferiority in their presence.

The clash of cultural values is present in other areas. White employers often complain about the Eskimo's lack of job stability:

> Many Eskimo, after working for several months, say they want to take time off to go hunting or to visit relatives in another village. Some will just quit outright when the hunting season comes along. While they are good workers for short periods, we have a hard time keeping them on month after month.

Others comment on the problem of dependency. "These people don't want to work. Some give up jobs in order to qualify for welfare"; or "Many Eskimo seem apathetic; they no longer want to go out and hunt, preferring instead to live off relatives who have a steady job."

Eskimo, on the other hand, frequently speak of discrimination on the job and in white recreational centers. Although hesitant to speak openly, they are nevertheless well aware of other more subtle forms of disparagement, such as the white man's disregard for village norms and rules concerning admittance to Eskimo social and cremonial functions, drinking, the curfew, and culling sexual favors from women.

In elaborating these problems, there is a tendency to lose sight of the tremendous scope of the changes the Barrow Eskimo have accomplished in one generation. To some whites, the village is an economic and socially depressed community, composed of poorly educated, dependent people who "don't know where they are going." To others, the community appears vibrant with activity, its leaders tackling the problems before them with zest and determination. Neither of these two pictures of Barrow are accurate, but both contain certain truths. Even with all its problems of modernization and social upheaval, Barrow is not severely disorganized. On the contrary, the fact that it is becoming more consciously aware of what its problems are, and how it should go about trying to solve them as a community, suggests a new level of growth and achievement. Of fundamental importance is the fact that the Eskimo like to live in Barrow. Its life is new and challenging, particularly for the young adults. There are more health, educational, and other services available. A new high school is being built there, and young and old alike now place a very high value on education. For the teen-agers, Barrow presents a level of sophistication unheard of in the smaller villages. In the summer of 1965, the ten-thirty P.M. curfew was not enforced, and Barrow youths spent much of the evening dancing the latest steps popular in New York and San Francisco discotheques. What was the favorite dance music? "Oh, anything that's good for dancing, the jerk, the monkey, the jitterbug, and the slow dance. Some do the twist."

A new bank opened in 1962 and within the past three years more than 400 people have established savings accounts. The bank also has granted loans of up to $8000 for building houses. The Eskimo rapidly are learning the advantages of savings, the techniques of applying political pressure to achieve greater government assistance, the value of a higher education, and the importance of organized recreation for the many young people who return home from boarding schools each summer. These efforts, along with the establishment of the intervillage annual *Innupiak* conferences, suggest that the community members are striving toward a new level of integration far more complex than that characterized by the traditional kin-based social structure of a generation ago.

The Quest for Identity

Although we have gained an understanding of the type and extent of social and cultural change that has taken place among the north Alaskan Eskimo, there still remains the question of the effect these changes have had on the Eskimo's self-image. Are the many Eskimo who adopt Western forms of behavior complying with the implied wishes of whites in order to better achieve their traditional goals? Do many Eskimo make use of Western materials, foods, and services because these items make life easier, without this adaptation's affecting their self-image? Or do these actions reflect a new self-identification in which they see themselves as part of the Western world? Given the difficulty of objectively delineating motivations behind actions, the proposed answers to these questions are tentative and open to further investigation. Nevertheless, some insights are available.

Compliance as a motivation for adopting Western-oriented behavior occasionally is observed among Eskimo men working for white employers. These men quickly learn how much effort to apply to a given task in a specific period of time and they follow this pattern, although in their own village some will speak of how lazy whites are or how little work they accomplish in a given day. These Eskimo have learned the importance of "exact" time and follow a schedule that would be considered meaningless in the context of their traditional village life. They also know, however, that if the work schedule is not followed, they will eventually be fired and thereupon lose their access to the desired cash income.

Other examples of compliance appear when Eskimo and whites mix socially. Some Eskimo will act like whites at a Saturday night radar station party, but, on returning to their village, may mimic the very behavior they exhibited a few hours earlier. In each of these illustrations, Western behavior patterns are adopted either to avoid certain punishments or to gain certain rewards, but there is little evidence to suggest that these responses reflect any important change in self-identification.

Nor do the adoption of Western technology and social institutions necessarily imply an important shift in Eskimo self-identification. Most Eskimo are quite pragmatic about the effectiveness of a given tool or idea, and accept or reject it according to their views of its usefulness. The outboard motor replaced the paddle and sail many years ago. Recently, a mechanical snowmobile was tried in Kaktovik, as a substitute for the dog team, until it became clear that the former was far less reliable than the latter as a means of transportation.

It is important to note, however, that the north Alaskan Eskimo have become dependent on items of Western technology and social institutions. Regardless of whether these items originally were adopted to fulfill traditional or Western goals, the decision to use fuel oil for heat, electricity for light, canned goods for food, manufactured suits and jackets for clothing, and clinic and hospital for medical care makes it increasingly difficult to separate one's image of oneself from the outside world on which so much depends. This realization is explicit among those Eskimo who, at a cost of much emotional and financial hardship, have decided to send their teen-age children away for further schooling. When asked why, a typical response of an Eskimo father was: "We different now. We no longer live old Eskimo way."

Hughes (1958:27) in a related discussion of the Eskimo on Saint Lawrence Island, Alaska, states the difference succinctly:

> It is one thing if a group of people are only using and assimilating as their own the manufactures and external paraphernalia of an outside

group with whom they happen to be in contact. It is quite a different matter if they begin to feel that they no longer want to be thought of or to think of themselves as belonging to their original group and rather conceive that they are part of an outside group. At such a point, a watershed has been crossed in the process of psychocultural change.

We may say, therefore, that a change in identification takes place when an Eskimo or group of Eskimo adopt Western forms of behavior because this behavior is attractive to them; that is, it is valued by them. In this sense, identification differs from compliance, where the individual or group acts like the outsider simply to gain favor or personal advantage, without there being any effect on the value system. Thus, for example, an Eskimo who identifies with whites often dresses like them to maintain the pleasing self-image this action provides him even though in some instances such clothing is inferior to traditional wearing apparel. This shift in identification is becoming increasingly common in north Alaska. Women who wear high-heeled shoes and Western skirts, men who participate in the activities of the National Guard, listen regularly to radio news broadcasts, attend local village affairs in suit and tie, and teen-agers who know all the latest hair styles, dance steps, and hit songs are all familiar sights. The fact that such activities take place in the villages and are, therefore, usually not observable to whites, suggests that compliance is not a motive underlying this behavior. Eskimo who choose to participate in Western-oriented forms of activity are not gaining any direct practical advantage from an outside group, nor are they forced to undertake this action. They do so because it is pleasing to them.

Support for this assumption comes from other Alaskan research. In Berreman's recent study of the Aleut Eskimo, he distinguishes between white valuation and identification groups and states:

> In the process of judging themselves by White men's standards, Aleuts are led to adopt many of the White men's values, perspectives and behaviors. Some individuals, and in some limited contexts all individuals, play the role of the White man, that is, they actually act "White." Therefore, White men on occasion seem also to constitute an identification group for the Aleuts since an identification group is one which, whether the individual belongs or not, provides his major perspectives and values. (1964:233)

How does this process take place?

Identity Change

Identity change first requires that an individual become dissatisfied with his traditional image of himself. This may occur when Eskimo, working with whites, find they do not have the knowledge to solve a particular problem. In classrooms, children may be discouraged from speaking their native language; teachers may criticize their lack of cleanliness or poor work habits. Older teen-agers may laugh at a twelve year old imitating a traditional dance movement, saying, "You're a dumb Eskimo." Mothers may be politely advised to change their techniques of processing food by a visiting public health nurse or dietetic expert. In these and numerous other situations the Eskimo must re-examine his traditional outlook or re-evaluate his capabilities.

If he becomes sufficiently dissatisfied with his present self-image he may undertake to change it. He can accomplish this in several ways. The Eskimo may destroy or give away those material objects with which he has been identified in the past. The hunter who sells or gives away his sled dogs is not only unable to hunt in the winter, but he is symbolically demonstrating to himself and those around him that he is a different person. He may attempt to reinforce this new image by changing his style of clothing, physical mannerisms, and speech habits, and in so doing, encourage others to treat or regard him in a different light. At Kaktovik, many of the Western-oriented women have a minimal knowledge of English vocabulary and grammar, yet they often use the little they know in conjunction with Eskimo in the same sentence or even in the same word, as "You gonna go *kuvuriak?*" (check the fish net); "He's *kuvuriak*ing"; "Don't *pakak*" (touch); or "Bring the *uluaraks*" (*ulu* women's knives). At Wainwright, on the other hand, where over fifty years of local schooling have given many more Eskimo a good command of English, only one language is spoken at a time depending on the person's preference and sense of identity.

An example of this commitment to change one's identity may be seen in the comments and actions of a middle-aged Kaktovik Eskimo who once said: "I never want to go back to the old way. It was too hard. I have a good job now. Always, there is food coming in. This is much better." This Eskimo was one of the first to take an eighteen-month work contract at the nearby radar site. The transition was difficult, for in committing himself to this new job he had to reject many of his old ways of thinking and behaving. The terms of his contract did not allow him to take time off for hunting, to move to his fish camp in the summer, or to travel to other villages to visit relatives. Nor could he actively participate in many of the traditional forms of sharing and cooperative exchange. Working under a white employer, he often felt ambivalent when other Eskimo spoke critically of white foremen, and on the job, he felt self-conscious and insecure in his relations with whites.

During this period of stress, he withdrew from most social contact in the village, spending evenings alone or with his wife and family in his home. On one occasion at work he was asked by other Eskimo to assist them in the completion of a task, but he declined saying he had his own work to complete. Then, as he became more proficient in his job, he gained more confidence as well as greater acceptance by local whites. The site chief spoke highly of him saying he was a steady worker who could be counted on to do the job assigned to him. A few months later, he began to take a more active part in community life. Armed with a new feeling of self-confidence, he participated in village recreation, worked to improve the church building, and in other ways attempted to reintegrate himself into the local social life. His acceptance was symbolized by his being voted a place on the village council, an action that might not have happened earlier since he had been an average hunter, at best.

From this brief portrayal, four extremely important facts emerge. First, successful identity change requires that one feel dissatisfied with one's traditional identity. Second, there must be sufficient motivation (that is, dissatisfaction with the old and appeal of the new) for the individual to want to bring about a change. Third, there must be adequate mastery of the roles associated with the new identity. And fourth, the new identity must be accepted by others held in esteem by the individual concerned.

Many Eskimo already have experienced the first two steps of this process. It is most pronounced among the school age and young adult population, but characteristic of others as well. The barriers to successful completion of identity change are found at the third and fourth stages. Lack of knowledge and insufficient training and experience in the ways of the outside world keep many Eskimo from mastering the new roles which signify the identity they want to achieve. Of course, in those instances where these roles are mastered, the individual may still face the further problem of possible alienation from other Eskimo, whites, or both.

Personality Adjustment

In an attempt to gather more specific information on this problem, the author undertook in 1960–1961 a specialized study of identity change and personality adjustment. Kaktovik was chosen as the site for the research since the lack of social disruption in the village made it possible for the investigator to bypass the problem of the extent to which social disorganization could influence the amount of personality adjustment.

The research had three aims: first, to determine the extent of Eskimo-white contact that had taken place among the village residents (providing at least a rough measure of the amount of exchange of cultural ideas that enabled the Eskimo to have a greater understanding of the white man's way of life); second, to determine the extent to which this contact had brought about a shift in Eskimo identification toward a more Western orientation; and third, to determine the degree of personality adjustment of the residents.

Bearing in mind the factors leading to positive identity change, it was hypothesized that those Eskimo who had relatively little contact with Western society and yet were strongly identified with that society would show more symptoms of personality maladjustment than would those Eskimo who had a greater amount of intercultural contact, regardless of whether or not they identified with Western society. In other words, even where newly defined economic and social goals could be attained (an important finding of the earlier study), the stresses placed on those Eskimo whose Western identification was greater than their understanding of Western society, would cause more symptoms of psychic distress than they would among a culturally comparable group whose modern knowledge enabled them to feel more secure in their identification. Furthermore, it was felt that those Eskimo who had extensive modern knowledge but who still chose to identify with their traditional way of life would show fewer symptoms of psychological maladjustment, which suggests that they had a realistic basis for their decision.

Indices used to determine the extent of white contact for each village resident included amount of formal education, knowledge of English, residential mobility with particular reference to urban centers, hospitalization, salaried employment, access to mass media such as radio, newspapers, and magazines, and National Guard or military service. Indices used to determine the extent of Western identification included preference for Western-oriented activities as opposed to traditional Eskimo activities such as games and dances, preference for Western foods versus caribou, uncooked fish, and other customary foods, and preferences for Western clothing and hair styles as opposed to traditional Eskimo styles. In each instance, an alternative was available for the preference listed. The degree of personality adjustment for each Eskimo was determined by use of a psychological questionnaire.

A detailed statement of the methodology used and results obtained is available in other publications (see Chance 1962; 1965; Chance and Foster 1962). Briefly, the results showed, however, that the Kaktovik women tended to have many more symptoms of emotional difficulty than the men, which probably reflected the greater stress placed on most of the women as a result of their loss of many traditional roles without adequate replacement, and the problems associated with their slower rate of acculturation as contrasted with that of the men.

Furthermore, when men and women were placed in distinct groups according to their degree of contact (high, medium, or low) and similar groups according to their degree of Western identification, those groups characterized by less contact then identification showed more symptoms of psychological disturbance than did groups whose contact and identification levels were the same, or whose Western identification was less than their level of white contact. Nor did demographic factors such as age, amount of education, marital status, ethnic descent, or number of kin in the village affect the rate of emotional disturbance; no correlations were found.

Finally, neither the degree of contact, nor the degree of Western identification, when considered by themselves, revealed significant differences with respect to psychological difficulty. Rather, it was the conflict described earlier—the commitment to change one's identity without an accompanying knowledge of the appropriate roles to play—that appeared conducive to emotional difficulty.

These results raise another question: how can a community like Kaktovik make a successful adjustment to rapid change on the social and cultural levels, when a significant segment of its population shows symptoms of maladjustment at the individual level?

First, while the symptoms were clearly present, the level of impairment did not appear to be at all severe. In fact, almost all village residents were able to carry out their daily tasks, participate in family and community affairs, and in other ways fulfill their varied responsibilities quite effectively, even if they showed these symptoms. Actually, one of the important findings to come from the study was not the high symptom rate present among many women but the lack of serious psychological impairment found among members of either sex. Although the women appeared to be experiencing more neurotic difficulties than the men, both appeared to be adjusting to their rapidly changing social environment quite well. During this phase of the study (1958–1961) only one individual was so psychologically incapacitated that she required the attention of other village members.

Second, Eskimo society tends to be male dominated. Most of the family and community decision makers are men. As long as these individuals are free from major psychological difficulties, they can serve as a powerful force in maintaining community integration (given sufficient feelings of self-respect and other conditions mentioned earlier in the chapter).

Finally, the most prevalent kind of symptoms found among Kaktovik women were those relating to feelings of inadequacy and tension. Although these symptoms were of obvious concern to those who exhibited them, there was little indication that they were of sufficient severity to affect the level of community integration—at least at that time.

In our analysis of the dynamics of change among the north Alaskan Eskimo, we began by focusing on the important social (that is, interpersonal) features of this process, including such factors as social mobility, communication, social control, goal attainability, value congruence, and intercultural relations. However, when studying people who are confronted with new opportunities requiring major alterations in behavior, it is also important to give attention to the intrapsychic forces operating within individuals. The results of the Kaktovik research, for example, would have been of minimal interest had single correlations been attempted between the degree of Western identification (that is, intrapsychic process) and personality adjustment, or between the amount of intercultural contact (that is, interpersonal process) and personality adjustment, for in neither instance was a correlation found. Only when each finding was compared with the other did a meaningful relationship with personality adjustment appear.

In conclusion, we see that, for the moment, north Alaskan Eskimo men tend to have greater access to the goals associated with modernization and Western identification and more opportunity to base their identification on a firm foundation than do the women. They are thus in a better position to adjust successfully to the requirements of the modern world. If, in the future, those women who have committed themselves to making a similar change are provided with a greater understanding and access to Western society, the differential rate of psychological difficulty should diminish. If, on the other hand, these symptoms continue among women, or new symptoms, due perhaps to the lack of acceptance by whites, appear among the men, pronounced repercussions in family and community life may result.

Future Government Policy

Since many Eskimo have assumed a greater Western orientation toward life, it is important to determine what implication this identity change has for government programs planned for the north. As everyone living in Alaska is aware, the geographical isolation of these villages is such that some form of government intervention in the economic, education, health, and welfare field will be needed for many years to come.

Essentially, state and federal government policy makers have three alternatives:[2] if they simply want to create a new set of conditions involving social or economic change to which the Eskimo must somehow adjust, then they may undertake the program without undue attention to the Eskimo's wishes. The recent tuberculosis control program is a fairly successful example, and the reindeer herding program, a less successful one.

If the government program is dependent on the wants and desires of the Eskimo, then they must tailor the program to fit Eskimo values and goals. It is at this point that the degree of shift in Eskimo self-image toward greater national consciousness becomes particularly significant since many of the government's goals are similar to those held by Western-oriented Eskimo, who hold increasing positions of leadership in community affairs. However, to the extent that the government attempts to force a prearranged program on the Eskimo without their support, a change is likely to occur, but not necessarily the one the government wants.

Third, if the government wants the Eskimo to change many of the conditions in which they live, then what the Eskimo wants necessarily dominates the success of the program. The "community action" section of the Economic Opportunity Act is based on this principle of self-help generated partly by outside funds and assistance.

Until recently, government efforts have tended to emphasize the development of physical and economic resources for the Eskimo. New schools have been built, health facilities have been expanded. Economic loans have been made to improve housing. Without belittling these efforts, it is nevertheless appropriate to ask whether permanent self-generated devel-

---

[2] The broad implications of these alternatives are discussed more fully in Goodenough (1963).

opment will be achieved by implementing these types of improvement programs alone? Are technical and economic assistance programs sufficient
conditions for the successful implementation of government policy of in-
tegrating the Eskimo into American society?

The answer depends, I think, on the characteristics of the group in
question. Where leadership patterns are well developed, where the population is basically literate, where there is a tradition of cooperation, where
organizations with legal powers to take action are available locally and
regionally, and where technical services are well developed and available,
programs of this sort can be quiet successful. When these characteristics
are not present, the programs will be less successful.

Most northern government workers are "program specialists" and
this makes sense when the problems are known. But the answers to many
social, economic, and psychological problems in the north have yet to be
worked out. Professional and technical knowledge and skills are essential
for effective development of the north, but they are not sufficient. It is
only when the government worker knows how to adapt this knowledge to
the economic, social, educational, and psychological realities of northern
populations—when he is able to think in terms of interlocking problems
as well as programs—that he can expect to be effective in aiding Eskimo
development in the north.

What is needed today is a program that will enable individuals at
all levels of the community to participate in the development of their
own resources. From a short-range point of view, it may be more efficient to give funds to build a technical school, health center, or construct
new roads. But if the Eskimo are to gain greater self-initiative, a greater
sense of personal worth, and a greater measure of control over their own
future, they must be included as active participants in the development
program. An increasing number of north Alaskan Eskimo are ready to undertake these efforts, as the recent *Innupiak* conferences have shown. The extent to which the government makes use of this potential will bear directly
on the success of its over-all policy.

7

The Old and the New

ATAATARURUG took careful aim with his boot and kicked a small stone over the edge of the cliff toward the sea below. The two of us were standing on the top of a high embankment several hundred yards from the village of Kaktovik overlooking the Beaufort Sea. The location was a favorite waiting place for Eskimo women whose husbands were out seal hunting, but today we were alone. It was cold and foggy, a typical September day. We both pulled our parka hoods up over our heads and sat down on a small knoll. Three years had passed since our first meeting and during the course of my fieldwork in the village we had come to know each other quite well.

"I am leaving soon," I remarked, stating the obvious. My bags and equipment had been packed for two days waiting for a break in the weather so a plane could come and pick me up. Perhaps today would mark my departure.

"Maybe you won't be back." The slightly higher inflection of the last word enabled me to interpret his statement as either question or fact.

"I'll be back, but I don't know when."

"Many *tanniks* come here. They stay for a little while, and then go home. We get a few letters and a Christmas card or two. Then we don't hear from them any more. Maybe you are like the others."

I waited for the reassuring phrase.

"I jokes," he said laughingly and gave me a slight jolt with his shoulder. "But I might not be here when you come back."

"Things will be different, I guess."

"They are different now."

I searched for the right words to ask the obvious question.

"Do you miss the old days, Ataatarurug?"

As usual, he answered by telling a story.

100

Ten years ago, Apik and I went on a trip to hunt the caribou. A day's ride from here a big storm came up. We knew it was going to be a bad one and I pointed my lead dog toward an old abandoned house nearby. Just then, Apik saw a caribou. We stopped and he killed it, but then it was too late to get to the house. The snow came down so thick we couldn't see anything. We had to make a snowhouse in the bank. We had meat, a small stove and tea, that's all. It was all right for a day or two, but the storm was so bad we could only get a little way toward home before the wind came up and we had to stop again. Pretty soon we run out of fuel. We jumped up and down and run around in our little house to keep warm. We think, we never get back to our home. But we went on. Next day we made it. Apik, he never liked to hunt after that. He works in Barrow now. But I don't think that old way is so bad. *Achu*. Anyway, people around here, they don't hunt so much any more. The young ones, they don't even know how.

While listening to Ataatarurug's story, I looked down along the beach and saw a middle-aged man and his wife gather up their rifles and gear, put them in their boat, and push off toward the lagoon. Noticing us on the bank, the man waved a greeting and then turned back to adjust his outboard motor.

"That's Tuligak. He always hunt when he can. His wife's a good shooter too. He's *innupiak*, a real Eskimo."

Feeling reflective, I had many questions to ask, but seemed unable to phrase them in a way that would be understandable to Ataatarurug. I felt him slipping away, the distance between us growing each minute we sat there. He seemed to feel it too, for he stood up, smiled briefly, and headed for his sister's house without a word.

As we look back over the history of the Eskimo, we see that for thousands of years their sense of identity as a group was strengthened by their ability to comprehend much of their own culture. With the exception

of some shamanistic knowledge and techniques, all aspects of the culture were known to its members. Today, as these Eskimo step into the modern world, their identity as "Eskimo" becomes weaker. It is no longer possible to make generalized statements about the Eskimo without introducing some degree of qualification—a characteristic applying to all peoples undergoing transition from one way of life to another.

What the future holds for the Eskimo largely depends on their own desires and goals and the opportunities for attainment, on their ability to better understand the world of which they are becoming a part through improved and advanced education and increased intercultural contact, and on their ability to maintain a sense of self-respect in situations which foster self-disparagement in relation to others more knowledgeable about the outside world.

Without idealizing the traditional way of life, one hopes that the personal qualities of resourcefulness, ingenuity, and good humor which have carried the Eskimo through many difficult periods in the past will not be lost as they make their way into the future.

Glossary

AANIGUTYAK: A special parturition lodge
ACHU: I don't know
AIPARIK: "The second," partners in spouse exchange
ANGAKOK: A shaman
ATIGI: A woman's long, fur-trimmed cloth parka
BELUGA: *Delphinapterus leucas,* a white dolphin, about ten feet long
HAKU: An Eskimo team game, the object of which is to make others laugh
INNUPIAT: The Eskimo; the genuine people
INYAKUNS: Little spirit people
IPAGAK: Play in the water
KARIGI: Men's ceremonial dance and club house
KUVURIAK: Check the fish net
MUKLUK: Fur and sealskin boots
MUKTUK: Whale skin, an Eskimo delicacy
NULUKATAK: Spring whale festival involving the traditional "blanket toss"
PAKAK: Get into mischief, touch
PUTIGAROK: A game of tag
QATANG: A reciprocal "kin" term for children of partners in spouse exchange
TANNIK: White man
TUNRAQ: An animal "helping spirit" accessible to a shaman
UGROOK: *Erignathus barbatus,* large bearded seal weighing up to 700 or 800 pounds
ULU: A woman's knife, shaped like a half-moon, with a bone handle
UMIAK: Large, open skin-covered boat used in hunting sea mammals

References Cited

ALASKA HEALTH SURVEY TEAM, *Alaska's Health: A Survey Report to the United States Department of the Interior.* Pittsburgh: Graduate School of Public Health, University of Pittsburgh, 1954.

BEECHEY, CAPT. F. W., R. N., *Narrative of a Voyage to the Pacific and Bering's Strait to Cooperate with the Polar Expeditions Performed in H.M.S. Blossom in the Years 1825, 1826, 1827 and 1828.* Philadelphia, 1832.

BERREMAN, GERALD D., Effects of a Technological Change in an Aleutian Village. *Arctic,* 1954, 7, 2, 102–107.

————, Aleut Reference Group Alienation, Mobility and Acculturation. *American Anthropologist,* 66:231–250, 1964.

BROWER, CHARLES D., *Fifty Years Below Zero.* New York: Dodd, Mead & Company, Inc., 1942.

CHANCE, NORMAN A., Culture Change and Integration: An Eskimo Example. *American Anthropologist,* 66:1028–1044, 1960.

————, Conceptual and Methodological Problems in Cross-Cultural Health Research. *The American Journal of Public Health,* 52:410–417, 1962.

————, Acculturation, Self-Identification and Personality Adjustment. *American Anthropologist,* 67:372–393, 1965.

————, and FOSTER, DOROTHY A., Symptom Formation and Patterns of Psychopathology in a Rapidly Changing Alaskan Eskimo Society. *Anthropological Papers of the University of Alaska,* 11(1):32–42, 1962.

GOODENOUGH, WARD, *Cooperation and Change.* New York: Russell Sage Foundation, 1963.

HUGHES, CHARLES C., The Patterning of Recent Cultural Change in a Siberian Eskimo Village. *The Journal of Social Issues,* 14:25–35, 1958.

LANTIS, MARGARET L., American Arctic Populations: Their Survival Problems. *Arctic Biology, 19th Biology Colloquium.* Corvallis: Oregon State College, 119–130, 1958.

————, Alaskan Eskimo Cultural Values. *Polar Notes,* 1:35–48, 1959.

MILAN, FREDERICK, *Observations on the Contemporary Eskimo of Wainwright, Alaska,* Alaskan Air Command, Technical Report 57–14. Fairbanks: Arctic Aeromedical Laboratory, 1958.

ROBERTS, PALMER W., Employment of Eskimos by the Navy at Point Barrow, Alaska. *Proceedings, Third Alaskan Science Conference,* 4–43, 1954.

SONNENFELD, J., An Arctic Reindeer Industry: Growth and Decline. *The Geographical Review,* XLIX, 1:76–94, 1959.

————, Changes in an Eskimo Hunting Technology, An Introduction to Implement Geography. *Annals of the Association of American Geographers,* 50:172–186, 1960.

SPENCER, ROBERT F., *The North Alaskan Eskimo, A Study in Ecology and Society,* Bureau of American Ethnology Bulletin 171. Washington, D.C.: U.S. Government Printing Office, 1959.

STEFANSSON, VILHJALMUR, *Arctic Manual.* New York: The Macmillan Company, 1944.

SWANTON, JOHN R., *The Indian Tribes of North America,* Bureau of American Ethnology, Bulletin 145. Washington, D.C.: U.S. Government Printing Office, 1952.

VANSTONE, JAMES W., A Successful Combination of Subsistence and Wage Economics on the Village Level. *Economic Development and Cultural Change,* 8:174–191, 1960.

————, *Point Hope, An Eskimo Village in Transition,* Publications of the American Ethnological Society. Seattle: University of Washington Press. 1962.

Recommended Reading

Many of the items among the references cited may be considered as recommended reading as well.

GUBSER, NICHOLAS J., *The Nunamiut Eskimos: Hunters of Caribou.* New Haven, Conn.: Yale University Press, 1965.
> A very fine contemporary description of the inland north Alaskan Eskimo of Anaktuvuk Pass.

HUGHES, CHARLES C., An Eskimo Village in the Modern World. Ithaca, N.Y.: Cornell University Press, 1960.
> An excellent contemporary account of the Eskimo of Saint Lawrence Island, Alaska.

————, Under Four Flags: Recent Culture Change Among the Eskimos. *Current Anthropology,* 6:3–69, 1965.
> A thorough and up-to-date survey of recent Eskimo culture change with commentaries by other Eskimo specialists. Excellent bibliography.

JENNESS, DIAMOND, *Eskimo Administration: Alaska.* Arctic Institute of North America, Technical Paper No. 10, 1962.
> A strongly worded but sympathetic review of the fortunes of the Alaskan Eskimo under the jurisdiction of the United States government from 1867 to 1960.

LANTIS, MARGARET, The Social Culture of the Nunivak Eskimo. *Transactions of the American Philosophical Society,* n.s., 35(3):156–323, 1946.
> A classic ethnographic study of a group of Bering Sea Eskimo.

————, *Alaskan Eskimo Ceremonialism,* Monograph of the American Ethnological Society, 11 Locust Valley, N.Y.: J. J. Augustin, Inc., 1947.
> A detailed and systematic account of traditional Eskimo ceremonial life.

MILAN, FREDERICK, *Observations on the Contemporary Eskimo of Wainwright, Alaska,* Alaskan Air Command, Technical Report 57–14. Fairbanks: Arctic Aeromedical Laboratory, 1958. Reprinted in *Anthropological Papers of the University of Alaska,* 11(2):1–108, 1964.

A brief but knowledgeable ethnography of this north Alaskan village.

OSWALT, WENDELL, *Napaskiak: An Alaskan Eskimo Community,* Tucson: The University of Arizona Press, 1963.

A study of contemporary village life of the Yupik-speaking Eskimo of the Kuskokwim River. Serves as an interesting contrast to the Eskimo of north Alaska.

SPENCER, ROBERT F., *The North Alaskan Eskimo, A Study in Ecology and Society,* Bureau of American Ethnology, Bulletin 171, Washington, D.C.: U.S. Government Printing Office, 1959.

A very thorough and scholarly portrayal of the traditional coastal and inland Eskimo of north Alaska. An indispensable background volume for studies of contemporary north Alaskan Eskimo ecology and society.

VALLEE, FRANK G., *Kabloona and Eskimo in the Central Keewatin,* Northern Coordination and Research Centre Report, Department of Northern Affairs and Natural Resources, Ottawa, 1962.

An extremely good study of recent culture change and interethnic relations among the Canadian Eskimo of Baker Lake, Keewatin District, Northwest Territories. Of particular value to the reader with comparative Eskimo interests.

VANSTONE, JAMES W., *Point Hope, An Eskimo Village in Transition,* Publications of the American Ethnological Society. Seattle: University of Washington Press, 1962.

An excellent study of the Point Hope Eskimo written by an anthropologist with many years of experience in the north.

WEYER, EDWARD M., *The Eskimos.* New Haven: Yale University Press, 1933.

A well-known general description of the Eskimo.